sheffield theatres
crucible lyceum studio

T0353196

STEEL

by Chris Bush

Thursday 13 September – Saturday 6 October 2018
Studio Theatre, Sheffield

STEEL
by Chris Bush

CAST (in alphabetical order)

IAN/DAI	**Nigel Betts**
VANESSA/JOSIE	**Rebecca Scroggs**

PRODUCTION TEAM

Director	**Rebecca Frecknall**
Designer	**Madeleine Girling**
Lighting Designer	**Jack Knowles**
Sound Designer	**James Frewer**
Casting Director	**Anna Cooper** CDG
Dialect Coach	**Michaela Kennen**
Assistant Director	**Ebe Bamgboye**
Making Room Observer Director	**Tommi Bryson**

Production Manager	**Stephanie Balmforth**
Stage Manager	**Sarah Gentle**
Deputy Stage Manager	**Lucy Topham**
Assistant Stage Manager	**Lizzie Laycock**

Thanks to

Cutler's Hall, Arnold Laver, Ian Whitehead, J&C Joel, Luke Child, RT Scenic, Sheffield Town Hall, Victoria Hall, Steel Deck and Hawthorn.

Cast biographies

NIGEL BETTS – IAN/DAI

Theatre credits include: *Albion* (Almeida); *Three Days in the Country* (National Theatre); *Wonderland* (Hampstead); *Pastoral* (Soho); *One Man, Two Guv'nors, War Horse* (National Theatre/West End); *Aladdin* (Lyric Hammersmith); *The 39 Steps, Up'n'Under, Henry IV* and *As You Like It* (West End); *Tinderbox* (Bush); *The Constant Couple, The Recruiting Officer* (Blue Eagle); *A New Way to Please You, Sejanus: His Fall, Thomas More, Night of the Soul* (Royal Shakespeare Company); *Eden End, Macbeth* (West Yorkshire Playhouse) and *Neville's Island* (Watford).

Television credits include: *EastEnders; Outlander; Little Boy Blue; Bliss; Bounty Hunters; Death in Paradise; Boy Meets Girl; Vera; Class; The Coroner; DCI Banks; New Tricks; You, Me & Them; The Wrong Mans; Class; Doctor Who; Waterloo Road; Doctors; Holby City; Downton Abbey; The Escape Artist; The Starlings; Doc Martin; Moving Wallpaper; The Bill; Trial and Retribution; The Catherine Tate Show; Coronation Street; The Street; Emmerdale; Grange Hill; Midsomer Murders; Silent Witness; Two Pints of Lager and a Packet of Crisps; Sharpe's Mission; Courtroom; Grease Monkeys; Inspector Lynley Mysteries; A Touch of Frost; Final Demand; Paradise Reclaimed* and *As Time Goes By.*

Film credits include: *David Copperfield; Undercliffe; The Christmas Candle; Lipstikka; Desert Flower; Mrs Ratcliffe's Revolution; In Your Dreams; Chain Male; Cheeky; Harold the Amazing Contortionist Pig; Keen Eddie* and *Thunderpants.*

REBECCA SCROGGS – VANNESSA/JOSIE

Theatre credits include: *What Shadows* (Birmingham Rep); *The Suicide, Danton's Death* (National Theatre); *One Monkey Don't Stop No Show* (Eclipse/Tricycle); *A Midsummer Night's Dream* (Filter/Lyric); *Dream Story* (Gate); *Doris Day, Fatal Light* (Clean Break) and *Detaining Justice* (Tricycle).

Television and radio credits include: *Flack; Casualty; Doctors; Holby City; EastEnders; Plenty More Fish; Death in Paradise; The Battle of Apemen* and *Cardboard Hearts.*

Production biographies

CHRIS BUSH – PLAYWRIGHT

Chris Bush is a Sheffield-born playwright, lyricist and theatre-maker.

For Sheffield Theatres credits include: *What We Wished For*, *A Dream*, *The Sheffield Mysteries* and *20 Tiny Plays about Sheffield*.

Other theatre credits include: *Pericles*, *A Declaration from the People* (National Theatre); *The Changing Room* (National Theatre Connections); *The Assassination of Katie Hopkins* (Theatr Clwyd); *Larksong* (New Vic); *Cards on the Table* (Royal Exchange Theatre, Manchester); *ODD* (Royal & Derngate: Concert Performance); *Sleight & Hand* (Summerhall/BBC Arts); *TONY! The Blair Musical* (York Theatre Royal/tour); *Poking the Bear*, *Speaking Freely* (Theatre503); *Wolf* (National Theatre Studio: Reading); *Scenes from the End of the World* (Royal Central School of Speech and Drama) and *The Bureau of Lost Things* (Theatre503/Rose Bruford).

Chris has been a resident artist for Sheffield Theatres and the Oxford Playhouse, and a member of the Orange Tree Theatre's Writers' Collective.

REBECCA FRECKNALL – DIRECTOR

Rebecca trained at Goldsmiths, LAMDA, and on the National Theatre Studio's Directors Course. She is Associate Director at the Almeida Theatre.

Theatre credits as Director include: *Summer and Smoke* (Almeida/West End); *Educating Rita* (Durham Gala); *Julie, What Are They Like?*, *Idomeneus* (Northern Stage); *You, Me, and Everything Else* (Soho/UK tour); *Aftermath* (Royal & Derngate); *A Streetcar Named Desire* (Young Vic/Parallel Production); *Something Cloudy, Something Clear* (Greenwich) and *Bassett* (New Diorama).

Theatre credits as Associate Director include: *Ink* (Almeida/West End).

Theatre credits as a Movement Director include: *Albion* (Almeida) and *The Wonderful Wizard of Oz* (Northern Stage).

MADELEINE GIRLING – DESIGNER

Madeleine trained at the Royal Welsh College of Music and Drama.

Theatre credits include: *The Importance of Being Earnest* (Set Design/Vaudeville); *Embrace* (Birmingham Royal Ballet/Sadler's Wells); *The Open House* (Costume Design. Ustinov Studio Bath/ Print Room); *The Weir* (English Touring Theatre); *The Shape of the Pain* (China Plate); *Go Between* (Young Vic); *Babe, the Sheep-Pig* (Polka Theatre/UK tour); *Rosencrantz and Guildenstern are Dead* (Shanghai Dramatic Arts Centre); *Always Orange*, *Fall of the Kingdom*, *Revolt. She Said. Revolt Again* (Traverse/Shoreditch Town Hall); *The Ant and the Cicada* (Royal Shakespeare Company); *Julie* (Northern Stage); *Right Now* (Ustinov Studio Bath/Bush/Traverse); *A Skull in Connemara*, *Arcadia*, *Time and the Conways* (Nottingham Playhouse); *The Harvest* (Ustinov Studio Bath/Soho); *Little Light* (Orange Tree); *The Chronicles of Kalki* (Gate); *Tender Napalm*, *How to Curse* (BOVTS); *Hey Diddle Diddle* (Bristol Old Vic) and *The Cagebirds* (LAMDA).

JACK KNOWLES – LIGHTING DESIGNER

Jack trained at the Central School of Speech and Drama.

Theatre credits include: *Good Vibrations* (Lyric, Belfast); *The Importance of Being Earnest* (Vaudeville); *Machinal, They Drink it in the Congo, Boy, Carmen Disruption, Game* (Almeida); *Happy Days, Parliament Square* (Bush); *Our Town, Twelfth Night, A Streetcar Named Desire, Wit, The Skriker, There Has Possibly Been An Incident* (Royal Exchange Theatre, Manchester); *Cave* (London Sinfonietta); *Dan and Phil: Interactive Introverts, The Amazing Tour is Not on Fire* (world tours); *Instructions for Correct Assembly, 2071* (Royal Court); *Caroline, or Change* (Chichester Festival Theatre/Hampstead); *Circle Mirror Transformation* (Home, Manchester); *Wonderland* (Nottingham Playhouse); *Beginning* (National Theatre/Ambassadors); *Barber Shop Chronicles* (National Theatre/ West Yorkshire Playhouse/Australian tour); *Committee* (Donmar Warehouse); *4.48 Psychosis, Reisende auf einem Bein, Happy Days* (Schauspielhaus, Hamburg); *Junkyard, Pygmalion* (Headlong); *Winter Solstice* (Actors Touring Company); *Watership Down* (Watermill); *The Forbidden Zone* (Salzburg Festival/Schaubühne, Berlin/Barbican); *Kenny Morgan* (Arcola); *The Massive Tragedy of Madame Bovary!* (Liverpool Everyman/Peepolykus); *Cleansed* (National Theatre); *The Haunting of Hill House* (Liverpool Playhouse); *Phaedra* (Enniskillen International Beckett Festival); *A Sorrow Beyond Dreams* (Vienna Burgtheater); *Lungs, Yellow Wallpaper* (Schaubühne, Berlin); *Moth* (Hightide/Bush); *Say it with Flowers* (Hampstead); *Night Train* (Schauspiel, Köln/Avignon Festival/ Theatertreffen); *In a Pickle* (Royal Shakespeare Company/Oily Cart); *Ring-A-Ding-Ding* (Unicorn/New Victory Theatre, New York/Oily Cart) and *Kubla Khan, Land of Lights, Light Show, There Was An Old Woman, The Bounce, Mr & Mrs Moon* (Oily Cart).

JAMES FREWER – SOUND DESIGNER

Artist of Middle Child, Boundless Theatre and Hull Truck.

Composition credits include: *One Life Stand* (Honeyblood); *I Hate Alone, All We Ever Wanted Was Everything* (Paines Plough); *Mercury Fur, Weekend Rockstars: An Album Play, Rapunzel, Sleeping Beauty, Cinderella, A Taste of Honey* (Hull Truck); *Modern Life Is Rubbish: A Musical Manifesto, Saturday Night, Sunday Morning* (Middle Child Theatre); *Mixtape* (Royal Exchange Theatre, Manchester); *The Hundred and One Dalmatians* (Birmingham Rep); *Twelfth Night* (Orange Tree); *Folk* (Birmingham Rep/Watford Palace/Hull Truck); *Get Carter* (Northern Stage/UK tour) and *The Thing About Psychopaths* (Red Ladder Theatre/national tour).

Musical Director and Performer credits include: *The Snow Queen* (New Vic); *Dancehall* (Cast Doncaster); *The Night Before Christmas* (Soho) and *This House* (National Theatre/dep performer).

Sound Design credits include: *The Season Ticket* (Pilot Theatre/Northern Stage); *This Land, Red Sky at Night* (Pentabus); *A Further Education, Deluge* (Hampstead); *Love Me Do* (Watford Palace Theatre) and *The Ugly Sisters* (Rash Dash/national tour).

ANNA COOPER cdg – CASTING DIRECTOR

For Sheffield Theatres credits include: *Love and Information*.

Theatre includes: *I And You, Dry Powder, Gloria* (Hampstead); *Circle Mirror Transformation* (HOME, Manchester); *Leave Taking, HIR* (Bush); *They Drink It In the Congo* (Almeida); *Five Finger Exercise* (Print Room); *Multitudes* (Tricycle); *A Number* (Young Vic/Nuffield); *Tonight at 8.30* (English Touring Theatre/Nuffield); *The Glass Menagerie, The Saints, The Snow Queen* (Nuffield); *The Hudsucker Proxy* (Liverpool Everyman/Nuffield); *The Arabian Nights* (Tricycle); *The Fastest Clock in the Universe, Lucky Seven* (Hampstead); *The Pitchfork Disney* (Arcola); *Jeffrey Bernard is Unwell* (Theatre Royal Bath); *Our Country's Good* (Liverpool Playhouse); *Scenes from an Execution* (Hackney Empire); *'Tis Pity She's a Whore* (Southwark Playhouse); *Ghosts* (West End) and *Measure for Measure* (Theatre Royal Plymouth).

Short film credits include: *The Knackerman; Bunny and Clive; That Woman* and *Act of Love*.

As Casting Associate, television credits include: *Manhunt; Capital; Doc Martin; Arthur & George; Silk; Atlantis; Ashes to Ashes; Vicious; The Politician's Husband; Mission Impossible 6; Dunkirk; Kursk; Where Hands Touch; The Lady in the Van; The Dark Knight Rises; Belle* and *Sex and Drugs and Rock 'n' Roll*.

MICHAELA KENNEN – DIALECT COACH

Previous work for Sheffield Theatres includes: *Everybody's Talking About Jamie* (and Apollo, West End) and *The Wizard of Oz*.

Theatre credits include: *Oslo*, *The Beaux Stratagem*, *The History Boys*, *Market Boy*, *Caroline or Change*, *Thérèse Raquin*, *The Alchemist*, *The Rose Tattoo*, *Playing with Fire* (National Theatre); *The Hypocrite*, *Hecuba*, *Oppenheimer* (Royal Shakespeare Company); *The Importance of Being Earnest* (Vaudeville); *Motown The Musical*, *Memphis The Musical*, *Hairspray* (Shaftesbury); *Neville's Island* (Duke of York's/Chichester); *South Downs/Browning Version* (Harold Pinter/Chichester Festival Theatre); *Chimerica* (Harold Pinter/Almeida); *Country Girl* (Apollo); *Butley* (Duchess); *Love Never Dies* (Adelphi); *Cabaret* (Lyric); *And Then There Were None* (Gielgud); *The Village* (Stratford East); *Abigail's Party* (Hornchurch); *Circle Mirror Transformation* (HOME, Manchester); *Summer and Smoke* (Duke of York's/Almeida); *Things of Dry Hours*, *The Brothers Size*, *Vernon God Little*, *The Glass Menagerie*, *The Government Inspector*, *Euridyce* (Young Vic); *Knives In Hens* (Donmar Warehouse); *Witness for the Prosecution* (County Hall, London); *One Monkey Don't Stop No Show* (Eclipse/Crucible); *Combustion* (Tara Arts); *Occupational Hazards* (Hampstead); *Future Conditional*, *The Crucible* (Old Vic); *The Believers* (Frantic Assembly); *Grounded* (Gate); *Adler & Gibb*, *The Nether*, *Routes*, *Truth & Reconciliation*, *Love, Love, Love*, *The Witness*, *The Victorian in the Wall* (Royal Court); *Jesus Jumped the A Train*, *Lovely and Misfit* (Trafalgar Studios); *Who's Afraid of Virginia Woolf*, *Oh, the Humanity* (Northern Stage); *Disgraced*, *Terre Haute*, *Artefacts*, *The Whiskey Taster* (Bush); *Damsel in Distress*, *She Loves Me* (Chichester Festival Theatre); *High School Musical 1&2* (Hammersmith Apollo/national tour); *Pagliacci* (English National Opera);

Film and television credits include: *Doctor Who*; *Odyssey* (pilot); *Grantchester*; *Midsomer Murders*; *Millie Inbetween*; *Cosi*; *Broken*; *Omar*; *Brimstone* and *Exam*.

EBE BAMGBOYE – ASSISTANT DIRECTOR

Ebe is a graduate from St Andrews University and an associate artist of the National Youth Theatre, having worked for them on twelve different projects. He is currently training under Matthew Xia on the Young Vic's directing mentorship programme.

Previous credits include: Observer Director for *Mountains* (Royal Exchange Theatre, Manchester) and Volunteer Assistant for *Zoetrope* (West Yorkshire Playhouse).

sheffield theatres
crucible lyceum studio

Sheffield Theatres is the largest producing theatre complex outside of London, home to three theatres: the Crucible, the Studio and the Lyceum. In recognition of its success in creating new work, its bold approach to new classics and accessible ticketing policy, the Theatre was named Regional Theatre of the Year 2017, by *The Stage*, for an unprecedented third time, adding to wins in 2013 and 2014. Sheffield Theatres has also celebrated exceptional success at the UK Theatre Awards over the last three years, winning a total of 12 awards. The 2017 UK Theatre Awards included two wins for *Everybody's Talking About Jamie*.

The company produces a diverse programme of work, spanning a range of genres: classical revivals, new work, large-scale musicals and innovative and immersive theatre experiences. It presents the best shows currently on tour in the UK and works with theatre artists locally and nationally to nurture and develop new creative talent.

Sheffield Theatres' 2018/19 season includes: *A Midsummer Night's Dream*, directed by Robert Hastie with music from co-creator of *Everybody's Talking About Jamie* Dan Gillespie Sells, co-production with Out of Joint *Close Quarters* by Kate Bowen directed by Kate Wasserberg, the riotous romantic musical comedy *Kiss Me, Kate* directed by Paul Foster and the world premiere of *Standing at the Sky's Edge* with music and lyrics by Richard Hawley.

Combining classic and contemporary programming with a bold and ambitious approach, Sheffield Theatres has firmly established itself as one of the country's leading theatres.

Staff

Chief Executive **Dan Bates**
Artistic Director **Robert Hastie**

Senior Management Team
Communications & Fundraising Director **Claire Murray**
Finance & Resources Director **Bookey Oshin**
Producer **Caroline Dyott**

Administration Team
HR Manager **Michael Bailey***
HR Officer **Lorna Knight**
Assistant to Chief Executive & Artistic Director **Jackie Pass**

Box Office Team
Sales & Customer Care Manager **Caroline Laurent**
Deputy Sales Managers **Kate Fisher, Louise Renwick**
Sales and Customer Care Supervisor **Claire Fletcher***
Access and Sales Supervisor **Paul Whitley**
Sales and Group Supervisor **Ian Caudwell***
Sales Assistants **Carrie Askew, Sue Cooper*, Alistair Eades, Sally Field, Faye Hardaker, Pat Holland*, Rebecca McQuillan, Christine Monaghan*, Christine Smith, Irene Stewart, Katy Wainwright, Hannah Winnell**

Communications Team
Communications Manager **Rachel Nutland**
Deputy Communications Manager **Oliver Eastwood**
Media Officer **Ellie Greenfield**
Communications Officers **Laura Bloor, Anna Lord**
Communications Officer (Maternity Cover) **Alice Dale**
Communications Trainee **Keir Shields**
Programmer **Mikey Cook**
National Press Support **Kate Morley PR**

Customer Services Team
General Bars & Catering Manager **Andrew Cooper***
House Manager **Debbie Smith***
Crucible Corner Manager **Kris Addy**
Head Chef **Natalie Bailey**
Sous Chef **Nathan Howe**
Chef De Partie **Daniel Lockwood**
Commis Chef **Antonio Massuno**
Kitchen Assistant **Dean Fox**
Apprentice Chef **Tom Jacobs**
Events Coordinator **Lianne Froggatt**
Events Management Trainee **Jasmine Chong**
Catering & Bars Shift Leaders **Aeddan Lockett, Archie Ward***
Café Supervisor **Joanne Murrison**
Duty Managers **Sue Cooper*, Andrea Eades, Lucy Hockney, Adrian Tolson, Tracy Waldron**
Firepersons **Denise Hobart, Suzanne Palzer, Lucy Procter, Heather Reynolds, Jon Robinson**
Cellar Person **Robin Atkinson**
Catering Assistants **Megan Archer, Carrie Askew, Rosy Asquith, Pippa Atkinson, Toni Brown, Caryl Carson, Jessica Chittenden, Leslie Cooper, James Doolan, Jenny Everson, Judi Flint, Alex Glentworth, Jess Goh, Joanne Hall, Molly Hayde, Christina Higgins, Nicole Hodder, Sandra Holmes, Juliet Ibberson, Lauren Jones, Sue Jones*, Holly Kempton, Helena Kinch, Gregory Knowles, Hannah Lamare, Lauren Lomas, Nuala Meely, Sarah Moat, Tom Nugent, Fabian O'Farrell, Lois Pearson, Ioana Radulescu, Cyndi Richardson, Abby Russell, Louise Sanderson, Liz Sayles, Richard Sidebottom, Harris Slater, Grace Parker-Slater, William Stroie, Andrea Suter, Claire Sweeney, Jonathon Syer, Rhiannon Weir, Jack Weston, Holly Williams, Annette Williamson, Isa Wood**

Front of House Assistants Anne Archer, Hester Astell, Steve Athey*, Courtney Ball, Belinda Beasley, Jean Bennett, Marianne Bolton, George Bowley, Mari Bullock, Ann Butler*, Julie Cartwright, Jane Challenger, Megan Clarke, Lilli Connelly, Vicky Cooper, Gillian Crossland, John Daggett, Marie Darling, Sandra Eddison, Maureen Foster, Emma Gibson, Sara Godbehere, Jake Goode, Nick Henry, Denise Hobart, Lucy Hockney, Abigail Ivall, Scott Johnson, Hannah Jones, Charlotte Keyworth, Beth Kinross, Alex Lamb, Martha Lamb, Diane Lilleyman, Margaret Lindley, Emma Lomas, Aimee Marshall, James Middleton, Sylvia Mortimer*, Susie Newman, Cat Oldham, Kourtney Owen, Liz Owen, Susanne Palzer, Jodie Passey, Ann Phenix, Nate Powell, Lucy Procter, Richard Rawson*, Heather Reynolds, Jonathan Robinson, Dionne Sulph, Adrian Tolson, Bev Turner, Tracy Waldron, Christine Wallace, Eleanor White, Joe White, Stuart Williamson*

Facilities Team
Buildings Manager **John Bates**
Buildings Officer **Rob Chapman**
Maintenance Supervisor **Julian Simpson***
Maintenance Technician **Richard Powell-Pepper**
House Assistants **David Hayes, Katie Howard, Amy Jenner, James McCready, Grace Staples-Burton, Jacob Ross, Kate Wilkinson, Richard Winks***
Receptionist/Telephonist **Angela Ridgeway***
Head Cleaners **Jenny Hardy*, Karen Walker***
Cleaners **Kelly Baxter, Susan Baxter, Tracey Bourabaa, Louisa Cottingham, Yvonne Dwyer*, Gail Fox, Jill Francis, Lynn Highton, Diane Sayles, Diane Turton, Andrew Wild**

Finance Team
Finance Managers **Stacey Colley, Samantha Pentland, Christine Drabble**
Finance Officer **Lesley Barkworth-Short***
Payroll & Finance Officer **Jean Deakin*,**
Finance Assistants **Lindsey Copley-Dunn, Faye Ellames**
Finance Trainee **Dami Fajinmi**

Fundraising Team
Fundraising Manager **Abigail Walton**
Individual Giving Officer **Leah Woffenden**
Individual Giving Officer (Interim) **Siobhan Halpin**
Membership Officer (Interim) **James Ashfield** (*This post is made possible by the Weston Jerwood Creative Bursaries programme*)

Learning Team
Creative Projects Manager **Emily Hutchinson**
Learning Project Worker – Education **Georgina Stone**
Fun Palaces Ambassador **Beverley Nunn**
Learning Workshop Assistants **Joe Barber, Tommi Bryson, Lois Pearson**

Author's Note

Why would anyone be a politician? That's one question at the heart of *Steel*. Are they all dedicated public servants or power-mad egomaniacs? Specifically, why would anyone go into local government, which can appear to be an endless cycle of changing nothing yet being blamed for everything? While there are certainly exceptions, we increasingly view those who seek public office with suspicion, and yet we do need someone in charge, don't we? Is the system rigged, or do we get the elected officials we deserve? If we're disappointed by our current crop, is it our fault for not taking more of an active interest? Perhaps it's actually the case that good deeds just go unnoticed – we only become aware of our politicians when they mess up.

Like most of us, I often feel infuriated by those in charge, and powerless as an individual to hold anyone to account, and yet I also feel some sympathy towards those who seem to be doing a mostly thankless, nigh-on-impossible job. This feels especially true of local government, where councillors don't even receive financial remuneration for their efforts (and perhaps, in some instances, we therefore get what we pay for). I imagine there are many occasions where being a politician can feel like a pretty wretched existence: the idealist in me would dearly like to believe most enter government with good intentions, but perhaps the constant need to compromise and placate will always take its toll.

In *Steel*, I want to try and show the people behind the rosettes – flawed and fallible, but human nonetheless. I also wanted to dig into what it takes to be a woman in the public eye, who, whatever their role, are held to an entirely different set of standards to their male counterparts. Josie and Vanessa are two very different people in different circumstances, and yet both find themselves struggling against a system that fundamentally wasn't designed for them. Through their journeys, the play asks why representation matters, how far we've come, and what we still have to achieve.

Chris Bush, September 2018

Acknowledgements

I'm hugely grateful to our whole brilliant team on this show, led by the phenomenal Rebecca Frecknall, and to Rebecca and Nigel for bringing these characters to life so beautifully. A big thanks too to Robert Hastie for saying yes, and letting this be one of his first ever commissions, and to everyone at Sheffield Theatres – making a show here always feels like a homecoming.

Additional thanks to Louisa Connolly-Burnham, Simon Rouse, Amanda Wilkin and Patrick Driver for early readings, Julie Dore, Andrew Gates, Sue Atkins and Lord Kerslake for taking the time to talk to me, Sarah Liisa Wilkinson and everyone at Nick Hern Books, and Julia, Alex and Matt at Berlin Associates.

C.B.

STEEL

Chris Bush

*For everyone who came before,
and everyone who'll come after*

Characters

1988

DAI GRIFFITHS, *fifties/sixties. Welsh. Seasoned Labour councillor. Member of cabinet for Business and Economy.*

JOSIE KIRKWOOD, *thirties. Local. Junior engineer at a local steelworks and Women's Officer for her union.*

2018

VANESSA GALLACHER, *thirties. Labour candidate for Metro Mayor. Born here, but has mostly lived in London. A former MP who lost her seat in 2017. Southern accent.*

IAN DARWENT, *fifties/sixties. Local. Deputy Leader of the Council. Vanessa's election officer.*

Actor playing Dai and Ian is white. Actor playing Josie and Vanessa is black.

Note on Text

A forward slash (/) indicates an overlap in dialogue where the next character starts speaking.

Author's Note

The piece takes place in a city unquestionably modelled on Sheffield, and references various real-world events, but the story is entirely fictional. No characters are based on any specific individuals.

This text went to press before the end of rehearsals and so may differ slightly from the play as performed.

ACT ONE

Scene One

2018. Outside the local Labour Party headquarters. IAN *waits.*
VANESSA *enters. There's a certain forced joviality on both parts.*

IAN. Vanessa!

VANESSA. Ian – hi!

> IAN *extends a hand, but* VANESSA *is going for the hug.*
> *A shuffling moment of awkwardness.*

Hah. Okay.

IAN. Sorry.

VANESSA. How about – ?

> *She goes for a kiss on the cheek instead. That's fine.* IAN
> *doesn't anticipate the second.*

Well. Um.

IAN. Very continental.

VANESSA. Thank God that's over.

IAN. You found us alright?

VANESSA (*a little surprised by the question*). I've been here
before.

IAN. You have?

VANESSA. Of course I have.

IAN. Right.

VANESSA. Must've been, I don't know, half a dozen times in
the last –

IAN. I wasn't suggesting –

VANESSA. You know it's actually not far from… I used to do
Woodcraft Folk, just round the corner, well, just down the –

IAN. Oh.

VANESSA. Back in the day.

IAN. Woodcraft Folk?

VANESSA. Yes.

IAN. That the one that's like hippy Scouts?

VANESSA. Something like that.

IAN. Very good.

VANESSA. Never really my… A bit too Kumbaya for my liking, but…

IAN. And you're well? You look well. Very –

VANESSA. Thanks.

IAN. Nice to see some people still make an effort.

VANESSA. Um. Thank you. I wasn't really… I just –

IAN. Nervous?

VANESSA (*surprised*). Nervous?

IAN. Don't be.

VANESSA. Oh, I'm not.

IAN. Right. Good.

VANESSA. I mean this is –

IAN. Yes.

VANESSA. Isn't it?

IAN. Hmm?

VANESSA. This is all… Look, I don't want to imply this is foregone conclusion, I don't want to be presumptive, but I am… I have been the, um, the presumptive candidate, in fact, for a while, if we used that term, haven't I? So –

IAN. Indeed.

VANESSA. And nothing's happened to…? Do you know something?

IAN. Rarely.

VANESSA. Right. (*Beat.*) But just to be clear, the situation hasn't…? You're not expecting any nasty surprises?

IAN. Not at all.

VANESSA. So why should I be nervous?

IAN. Sometimes people just get nervous.

VANESSA. Right.

IAN. But I can see you're not.

VANESSA. I wasn't.

IAN. My apologies.

VANESSA. It's fine. I'm fine. Sorry. You just gave me a little… Because I don't want to sound dismissive. Obviously the other candidates are both –

IAN. Obviously.

VANESSA. So I'm not –

IAN. Don't want to insult your sisters.

VANESSA (*forcing a laugh*). Hah. No.

IAN. And the sisters are particularly good at getting insulted. Carol practically makes a living from it.

VANESSA (*biting her tongue*). Hmm.

IAN. Sure everything's alright?

VANESSA. Yes. Yes, everything's… Actually no, sorry. Sorry, can I be an arsehole?

IAN. Uh…

VANESSSA. Sorry, but… No, actually, I'm not sorry and I'm not being an arsehole, this is actually a very… And I know you're one of the good guys –

IAN. Right.

VANESSA. But if you could not… That word. Can you not use that word, please?

IAN. Beg pardon?

VANESSA. The S word.

IAN. I'm not –

VANESSA. 'Sisters' – with that inflection, and that general…
Because look, it's bad enough when a woman says 'sisters'
about a group who aren't actually… I genuinely feel my
ovaries cringe every time I hear it, but when a man – and
I know you're not a… and look, hashtag-not-all-men and so
on, but when you refer to me and my fellow democratically
selected candidates as 'the sisters' it sort of makes me want
to put my fist through something.

IAN. Right.

VANESSA. Sorry.

IAN. Don't be.

VANESSA. No. Right. I'm not.

IAN. I'm sorry to –

VANESSA. As you should be. (*Beat.*) Joking – that was joking.
Only not really –

IAN. Understood.

VANESSA. Because we are… We're not a sorority, we're
serious political operatives, and it is a big deal, actually – to
have an all… And not an 'All-Women Shortlist' by design,
not because it was enforced, but a shortlist which happens to
be only –

IAN. Yes.

VANESSA. Because the best three candidates just happened to
be –

IAN. Absolutely.

VANESSA. Which is what happened.

IAN. No argument from me.

VANESSA. Each of us here on merit, each with our own…
Carol can moan, but her business record is exemplary, and

Deborah, well, Debbie is… the heart of the community, isn't she? The backbone of… Salt of the earth –

IAN. Both got a lot going for them.

VANESSA. And when I heard… I think we were all thrilled, weren't we? All so excited, because –

IAN. You knew you could beat them?

VANESSA. No! (*Beat.*) Well yes, but –

IAN *laughs*.

But not only because of that, because it represented a real… It shouldn't be remarkable, it shouldn't be remotely surprising, but these are milestones, they are, and they need to be celebrated, not derided, not treated with suspicion, or undermined by… I get enough of that from elsewhere.

IAN. Won't happen again.

VANESSA. Thanks. Thank you. (*Breathing, calming slightly.*) Look, let's just get through tonight, let's just… And it will be easier then, won't it?

IAN. How do you mean?

VANESSA. Once I'm… Presuming I'm… Once they're stuck with me. Because I can win over the public – I know how to do that, but it's you bastards who're the real… Sorry.

IAN. That's alright.

VANESSA. And I'm all for healthy debate, I am, and a rigorous, forthright… But it's exhausting – this has all just been very draining, actually, day after day, the three of us continually having to justify our collective existence, so after this evening I would really like to just be able to say, 'Look, this is who you've got, so fall in line.'

IAN. And I think people will. I think yes, to an extent…

VANESSA. Good. And I know – I do realise with all the… Tonight might not feel exactly like a coronation. I'm prepared for that.

IAN. You saw the email then?

VANESSA. What email?

IAN. The… Never mind.

VANESSA. What email?

IAN. Not important – we can talk about it later.

VANESSA. Ian –

IAN. It's nothing, it's… It's just a new email chain with a few idiots blowing off some steam.

VANESSA. Right.

IAN. Honestly –

VANESSA. Can I see it?

IAN. I'll show you after.

VANESSA. That bad?

IAN. No! (*Beat.*) Fine. Hang on.

> IAN *starts trying to find the email on his phone*.

VANESSA. Because this is exactly the… It's embarrassing – I'm actually just embarrassed by all of it – the pettiness, the squabbling, the continual –

IAN. Now just bear in mind –

VANESSA. I'm a big girl – please.

IAN (*passing his phone to* VANESSA). Alright.

VANESSA. Alright then. (*Scrolling through.*) '…high-handed interference from the NEC, forcing upon us…' well, naturally – 'a sordid selection process swaddled in scandal, secrecy and scurrilous self-interest…' You know that's Brian, he's the one who writes his own poetry.

IAN. Christ, don't remind me.

VANESSA. Oh, and here it is: 'instead of representing the true interests and values of the local party, we have become a Petri dish for political correctness and social engineering.' Jesus. It's not a dog whistle, it's an air-raid siren.

IAN. You've got to remember this is just a vocal minority.

VANESSA (*passing the phone back*). Who are these people? How do they think this is helping?

IAN. They're just a little stuck in their ways.

VANESSA. Unbelievable. Infants. That they're so threatened by… They need me. Do you have any idea how much they need me up here?

IAN. Everyone appreciates –

VANESSA. They don't! Ungrateful fuckers. They don't make it easy.

IAN. Alright, let's try not to –

VANESSA. Yes, yes, you're right. Okay then – let's get this shit-show over with.

VANESSA *leaves and* IAN *follows. We hear (but needn't see) the returning Officer announcing the results of the candidate vote.*

OFFICER. The total number of votes cast was four thousand, five hundred and eighty-five, representing a sixty-four-point-three-per-cent turnout. Two hundred and twenty-one votes were found to be invalid or spoilt, bringing the total number of eligible votes to four thousand, three hundred and sixty-four. They were cast as follows: In the first round, Gallacher, Vanessa: one thousand, nine hundred and thirty-three votes. Henshaw, Carol: one thousand, five hundred and forty-two votes. Lister, Deborah: eight hundred and eighty-nine votes. As there is no overall winner, Debbie's votes went to second preference. Four hundred and seventy-four of those went to Vanessa Gallacher, bringing her total to two thousand, four hundred and seven, and four hundred and fifteen to Carol Henshaw, coming to one thousand, nine hundred and fifty-seven. Therefore Vanessa Gallacher is duly elected as the Labour candidate for Metro Mayor.

The sound of applause, perhaps not exactly deafening.

Scene Two

1988. We're now inside a small meeting hall, where a CLP meeting has just finished. DAI, *a seasoned councillor, is with* JOSIE, *the evening's guest speaker.*

DAI. Can I just stop you there?

JOSIE. I didn't say anything.

DAI. But before you do –

JOSIE. I should... My bus is...

DAI. Can I just explain what I think happened?

JOSIE. Um...

DAI. Just to... Just because –

JOSIE. I was there, so –

DAI. Yes. No. Absolutely. But what I think is, I think you may have misinterpreted the, uh, the intent of –

JOSIE. It's fine.

DAI. You're upset.

JOSIE. I'm not.

DAI. It's fine to be upset, but I think if I just explained –

JOSIE. I'm really not.

DAI. Because it was a joke.

JOSIE. I know.

DAI. But I'm not sure you understood the... the... If I could just take a moment – please – if you'd indulge me?

JOSIE (*still somewhat reluctantly*). Of course.

DAI. Good. Excellent. Thank you. So the first thing to say is that we don't even have a tea lady.

JOSIE. Right.

DAI. We... So there could be no, no one was genuinely mistaking you for – nobody thought you were actually –

JOSIE. No.

DAI. Because we just sort ourselves out, you see? There isn't a... We have a biscuit rota. Sometimes one of the women bakes. (*Then immediately worried.*) And that isn't to say – not that... I do believe it is only the women who bake – in my experience of these particular meetings – but that isn't a... a... that's not a matter of policy. There's no expectation.

JOSIE. Of course.

DAI. Always very welcome, but –

JOSIE. Got it.

DAI. But – but yes – but my point is everyone did know who you were. You were on the agenda. Josie Kirkwood: British Steel.

JOSIE. I saw.

DAI. So. So. And here's where I think things got... The joke, as I understand it – and it was a joke – was look, here you are, guest speaker at your first constituency meeting, brilliant, um, brilliant mind, young blood, sister in solidarity and all that, and then, 'Oh no, what's this? Everyone thinks I'm the tea lady!'

JOSIE. Right.

DAI. Which is, yes, in itself isn't funny – unkind, maybe – but then, then it would become clear that was all just ribbing, just pulling your leg, and that would, you see, would put you at ease, funny because it's so ridiculous, the idea that any of us would... Shows we're all on the same side.

JOSIE. I see.

DAI. You do?

JOSIE. I do. I did. Honestly.

DAI. So it really was all just a... It is, I believe, it's just how they show their affection around here – it took me a while to get used to it.

JOSIE. Oh, I know. We give as good as we get.

DAI. Yes. Yes of course, and when I said… Yes, of course you're the local, not me – I didn't want to imply anything otherwise.

JOSIE. It's really fine.

DAI. Good. That's good. I'm glad.

JOSIE. You can't be a woman in steel without developing something of a thick skin.

DAI. I can imagine.

JOSIE. But I should probably –

DAI. I would just really hate to think of you leaving with the wrong impression.

JOSIE. Mr Griffiths –

DAI. Dai, please.

JOSIE. Dai – can I tell you what they said to me – what the foreman said to me on my very first day at the steelworks?

DAI. Please.

JOSIE. He said, 'Steel? Face that colour, I thought you'd come straight out of the mines.'

DAI. Oh. Oh, I…

JOSIE. So as first impressions go –

DAI. And that is… Believe me, I would never –

JOSIE. I'm saying it's fine. I'm saying jokes about being the tea lady pale in comparison.

DAI. Right.

JOSIE. No pun intended.

DAI. Hmm?

JOSIE. 'Pale', because… Doesn't matter.

DAI. Ah.

Pause.

Anyway… Anyway your talk was very… Truly powerful. Challenging but powerful. It was just what we needed.

JOSIE (*very much summing up*). My pleasure.

DAI. No, all mine, really. (*Beat.*) Sorry, there was just... There is one other thing, if you have the time.

JOSIE. Um –

DAI. It won't take a minute.

JOSIE. Sure.

DAI. Excellent. Yes, so again, tonight was really... A very different, a very exciting energy, I thought, in the room. And we are always looking for... young blood, fresh perspectives. I don't know if you heard, but there is an opening coming up here, shortly – locally.

JOSIE. An opening?

DAI. You do live in this ward, don't you? I know your father, his shop is –

JOSIE. Yes.

DAI. Is it something you'd given any thought to?

JOSIE. I'm sorry, is what something?

DAI. Standing – when Bill retires.

JOSIE. For the council?

DAI. And of course my seat's here too, so I'd be happy to talk you through any of the... the... I'd be in your corner.

JOSIE. Um... Right. Er...

DAI. You hadn't considered – ?

JOSIE. No. No, I genuinely... Not for a second.

DAI. But you are a Party member – and you're active in your union?

JOSIE. Yeah.

DAI. You have things to say, obviously.

JOSIE. I suppose, but... Yeah, on certain... But I'm not sure this is my natural –

DAI. How would you know?

JOSIE. Because I… Um, I guess I don't, really, but the
impression I get is… I want to say this carefully because
I don't want to cause offence and I'm sure – I know – what
you do here is, is… it does matter, it does have some impact –

DAI. But?

JOSIE. But… Yeah, I guess the 'but' is just whether this
environment is… uh…

DAI. Not quite your scene?

JOSIE. I'm very flattered.

DAI. It's alright.

JOSIE. But is this somewhere where I – where someone like
me…?

DAI. Yes. I'm afraid we are a little… pale, male and stale,
I believe the phrase is.

JOSIE. I didn't mean that.

DAI. No, I understand. Well, I thought at least I'd… Worth
a shot, anyway.

JOSIE. But it's so nice that you'd… Thank you, honestly.

DAI. Not at all. (*Beat.*) Who knows how we change that though.

JOSIE. Sorry?

DAI. Sorry – you needed to get off.

JOSIE. Yeah, I… (*Checking watch.*) Doesn't matter, it's not far
to walk.

DAI. Oh no, have I – ?

JOSIE. It's fine, really.

DAI. I do go on.

JOSIE. But you were saying? Change what?

DAI. Oh, it's… Yes, well it's the problem I've been struggling
with – that a number of us – of the more enlightened… How
do you make this a more appealing environment to begin with
for those people who will, ultimately through their very

presence, make the environment more appealing? And, and yes, there is a school of thought that says decisions are made by the people who show up, and we shouldn't be going out of our way to… If they're not interested, that's their loss. But I don't think that's fair. I don't think it's accurate. I don't think they're uninterested, I think they're put off by, by, by the very design of places like this – the smoke-filled backrooms and sticky floors. And that will change – it will change as our make-up changes – but the question, the challenge, is how can we coax those first few people through the doors?

Beat.

JOSIE. Right.

DAI. Anyway. Not to worry.

JOSIE. Sure.

DAI. I have my car – can I drop you somewhere? Where are you heading?

JOSIE. What would I need to do?

DAI. I'm not… I don't want petrol money or anything.

JOSIE. To stand – if I was interested in standing?

DAI. Oh.

JOSIE. Not saying that I am.

DAI. Right.

JOSIE. Not necessarily. But just out of –

DAI. Right. Right, yes. Well it's all very straightforward, very simple. There's a form – I can talk you through it – then a little chat – just to make sure you don't have any particularly ghastly skeletons in your closet. All very informal. In fact I recommend not taking any of it too seriously. Not *un*seriously, but just to keep it all quite light, actually, show them you can have a laugh – you have a sense of humour –

JOSIE. That I can take a joke?

DAI. I… Yes. And again I will apologise about earlier if you did feel –

JOSIE. Please don't.

DAI. But yes, people respond to… If you show you can play nicely with others –

JOSIE. Got it. I can do that. And I can be funny. I can do jokes.

DAI. Great stuff.

JOSIE. I can… Not that I'm committing – but I will have a think – I will give it some serious thought, and – not *too* serious, mind, but I will… Yeah. I've got a lot to – it's a lot to process, but… Yeah. No. Good. That's all good.

DAI. Smashing.

JOSIE. But right now I should –

DAI. Of course. Sure you don't want a lift somewhere?

JOSIE. No, I'll be fine, thank you. I think some air would…

DAI. As you wish. Well then. (*Offers his hand, slightly awkwardly.*) Miss Kirkwood, welcome to the council.

Scene ends.

Scene Three

2018. IAN *greets* VANESSA. *She has with her a large refillable coffee cup.*

IAN. Madam Mayor!

VANESSA. Alright, let's not get… One step at a time.

IAN. Absolutely. Still, got what we needed – and all without too much unpleasantness.

VANESSA. And only two hundred spoilt ballots.

IAN. Don't worry about that. Onwards and upwards.

VANESSA. Exactly. Next step – top of the agenda – crush the saboteurs.

Beat.

IAN. Right.

VANESSA. I'm joking – Jesus!

IAN. Alright.

VANESSA. Your face.

IAN. I just think… even in private we should avoid drawing any comparison between –

VANESSA. Oh really?

IAN. I just –

VANESSA. That wouldn't be a vote-winner?

IAN. Maybe not.

VANESSA. And that's a comparison a lot of people have been drawing, is it?

IAN. I didn't say that.

VANESSA. I mean I do still intend to crush them – if they're not suitably crushed already.

IAN. Let's not get –

VANESSA. Because seriously, the constant infighting within the various enclaves of the Judean People's Front that is the Labour Party does make me want to open up a vein, but now I've actually won, I say let's nail the fuckers.

IAN. Right.

VANESSA. That's a Monty Python reference, just for the record, not antisemitism.

IAN. Yes.

VANESSA. Because you can't be too careful these days, can you?

IAN (*gesturing to the coffee*). Not your first of the morning?

VANESSA. Hmm? No, no. No, I'm full of beans. I've got one of the, the little – the pod machines, y'know? The capsules – the automatic – godsend. Because I'm not being funny, but half the places you go into here, you ask for a soya latte and they look at you like you've pissed on their parkin, so…

IAN. Right.

VANESSA. You know what I mean?

IAN. I'm more of a Yorkshire Tea man myself.

VANESSA. Ah yes, of course, very on-brand.

IAN. Anyway –

VANESSA. Sorry, that was really obnoxious.

IAN. No –

VANESSA. No, it was, and here's the thing – let London have its wanky coffee. I want the tea. I want the pies. I want the chips cooked in dripping. That's who I really am – that's what I was brought up on.

IAN. Yes.

VANESSA. That is… You should be writing that down actually, because that's my narrative. This is my homecoming.

IAN. Yes. (*Beat.*) Only the issue is –

VANESSA. Perception. It's about perception, that's all. And this is where we – where *I* – we've all failed to… They don't realise I'm one of them.

IAN. Now there's a little truth in… But you are, to be fair, a relatively new addition to, to the landscape –

VANESSA. I was born here.

IAN. The *political* landscape.

VANESSA. Just because my parents were dirty southerners, that doesn't mean –

IAN. No.

VANESSA. Or are you getting at something else?

IAN. All I mean is –

VANESSA. Jerry Allen turned his back on me when they announced the vote. He literally turned his back.

IAN. Most I've seen him move in years.

VANESSA. A former Party Treasurer.

IAN. It's... Yes. Disappointing.

VANESSA. One word for it.

IAN. Jerry is... passionate. A bit of a hothead, but his commitment –

VANESSA. Jerry Allen is a crybaby and a bully who doesn't like being told no.

IAN. He only wants what's best – what he considers to be best for the party.

VANESSA (*reading from her phone*). '@Vanessa4MetroMayor needs to get back to where she came from.'

IAN. Jerry's not – ?

VANESSA. No. (*Checks.*) 'EricTheRed66'. Anonymous Twitter troll. Actually far more polite than most.

IAN. And that is unacceptable, and we will –

VANESSA. Where do you think they mean, exactly?

IAN. I'm sorry?

VANESSA. That I should be getting back to? I mean are we just talking Islington, or are they going full Bongo-Bongo Land?

IAN. It sickens me, it does, and anything I can do to –

VANESSA. You can challenge the narrative.

IAN. Right.

VANESSA. That I don't belong here. That this isn't home.

IAN. Yes, I do see that, only –

VANESSA. That this can't be home for people like me.

IAN. No, and it isn't... I honestly don't think it's a race thing, not for the vast majority of... I think entirely separately, some people have qualms about your, your route here –

VANESSA. Qualms?

IAN. And I'm not saying they're justified –

VANESSA. I wasn't dropped in. This isn't parachuting.

IAN. No.

VANESSA. I am a prodigal daughter. Yes, I moved away. In order to, to… to gain experience, to seek my fortune in the big city, and that is why, actually – that's why I beat Carol, who's never set foot inside Westminster, and Debbie, bless her, who's never been south of Derby. That's critical.

IAN. I agree.

VANESSA. And actually, actually losing my seat in the Commons last year, that was – it was tough, yes, it was character-building, it was a learning experience – but it was in truth the best thing that could've happened to me, because it meant I got to come back here – I got to do this – I got to come *home*.

IAN. Right.

VANESSA. Because this is where I need to be. It's not a back-up plan, it's not my consolation prize, it's bigger than any… The Metro Mayors are a fundamental shift in the power dynamic. This is a grassroots revolution in local governance.

IAN. Yes, I think I got that memo too.

VANESSA. I mean it. And I've got plans – big plans for this city – plans like you wouldn't believe. When I'm Mayor –

IAN. Now who's getting carried away?

VANESSA. Okay, okay, but I am the Labour Party candidate and look at where we are, so hello! I am the Labour Party candidate whether Jerry Allen and all his little gammon-faced, pin-dick friends like it or not.

IAN. And seeing as you are, perhaps you could extend an olive branch to –

VANESSA. And seeing as I am, perhaps they could form an orderly queue to kiss my arse.

IAN. Have you given much thought to decaf?

VANESSA. I am the Labour Party candidate. Now ask me why.

IAN. Why?

VANESSA. Because I am the best damn person for the job. Now ask me why again.

IAN. Why?

VANESSA. Because I belong here.

IAN. Right.

VANESSA. I belong here, and we are going to make sure everybody knows it. No one's going to make me look like an idiot.

Scene ends.

Scene Four

1988. JOSIE *has just come from her selection interview. For some reason she wears an apron and hairnet akin to Mrs Overall from* Acorn Antiques *and holds a tea tray. She is clearly upset, and* DAI *is trying to calm her.*

DAI. So. So okay. So that was… I'm not entirely sure what that was, but –

JOSIE. Don't.

DAI. But a very spirited, uh –

JOSIE. Your idea.

DAI. I'm sorry?

JOSIE. This – all this – this was your –

DAI. Uh –

JOSIE. Show them you're a laugh. Show a sense of humour.

DAI. I'm not sure I followed –

She rattles the tray, impersonating Julie Walters.

JOSIE. 'Two soups!'

DAI. Who is it again?

JOSIE. Mrs Overall!

DAI (*still blank*). Right.

JOSIE. Julie Walters!

DAI. Okay.

JOSIE. Tea lady. She's a funny tea lady, that's her thing, so after the whole… I was referencing – I was playing on their… I was being in on the joke.

DAI. I see.

JOSIE. Like you told me.

DAI. You did make quite a mess.

JOSIE. That's what she does!

DAI. Right.

JOSIE. That's why it's funny!

DAI. Understood.

JOSIE. She does this walk with the… She… She has this tray, and…

DAI. And she's on the television, is she?

> JOSIE *lets out a moan.*

> I'm just trying to –

JOSIE. Yes! Yes, she's a funny tea lady off the telly, so I thought – I thought it would be a nice idea to… I had a speech and everything, I'd planned a… After I'd, I'd broken the ice, I'd won them over –

DAI. Right.

JOSIE. I was going to talk about tea – about how tea is the most quintessentially English thing you can imagine, right? Except it isn't – it's from China, it's from India, it's from the Orient, it's fuelled empires and trade wars and sparked revolution, and, and… but it is, it still is the most quintessentially English thing, because we made it ours. Because we – we British are at our best not as colonisers but as magpies – this tiny island that takes the best the world has to offer and finds a new home for it

– makes it our own. And that is what we must keep doing, because that is what we've always done – that's how we got here. A cup of tea was at one point the most unusual, most exotic, the most foreign thing I could've shown you, and now it's the very emblem of our nation – something we cannot live without. So I am proud to be your tea lady, because tea ladies are the harbingers of the revolution!

DAI. Right. Golly. Well that's –

JOSIE. In closing – in closing, gentlemen, I'd say – I'd like to quote Eleanor Roosevelt. Eleanor Roosevelt said 'A woman is like a tea bag: you can't tell how strong she is until you put her in hot water.' Well, I'm more than used to a bit of heat, and I'm confident I'm strong enough for anything this role can throw at me.

Pause.

You hate it.

DAI. No! No, I imagine if you'd said any of that it would've gone down rather well.

JOSIE. Ugh!

DAI. It's alright.

JOSIE. No it isn't.

DAI. I don't think it was as bad as you think it was.

JOSIE. Forget it. No – you're right – we should forget all about it.

DAI. I didn't say that.

JOSIE. I never wanted this anyway – this was your idea. And I told you, I told you it wasn't for me, but you pushed and you pushed and –

DAI. Josie –

JOSIE. And you got in my head –

DAI. Please –

JOSIE. And you told me it would be straightforward.

DAI. And – yes, and just to… In my defence I do believe you might've overcomplicated things.

JOSIE. I like to plan ahead.

DAI. Yes.

JOSIE. I put a lot of thought into this.

DAI. I can tell.

JOSIE. Please don't make fun of me.

DAI. I'm not – I promise I'm not. I see how all this was… I see the effort that you've… (*Beat.*) Can I ask you one thing?

JOSIE. What?

DAI. Why is a tea lady carrying soup?

A pause. JOSIE realises he's right. She lets out an audible groan. She might cry. She is exhausted.

Sorry.

JOSIE. Oh God.

DAI. I shouldn't have said anything.

JOSIE. She isn't… Two Soups is a waitress, Mrs Overall is a different…

DAI. So perhaps –

JOSIE. Stupid. I'm stupid. They all must think I'm so stupid.

DAI. Nobody thinks that.

JOSIE. Well they should.

DAI. Spirited. Memorable –

JOSIE. Look at me! (*Looks down at herself.*) Why am I still wearing this? (*Tears off the apron.*) Like a… Like a joke, like I think it's all some big… And I don't. I want this – I really want it.

DAI. I know.

JOSIE. I didn't before, but now… I do this, I get inside my head, I fixate, I overthink and I lose sight of –

DAI. It's okay.

JOSIE. How is this okay? I had one chance – one opportunity to show I was competent and professional or at least not mentally deranged and instead I turn up looking like this and I throw cream of leek all over them –

DAI. I think... it was a smattering at most.

JOSIE. It isn't funny! It isn't to me!

DAI. It's fine.

JOSIE. No it isn't. (*Beat.*) I need to go back in – can I go back in? Can I talk to them, or write to them to apologise? I need to –

DAI. There's no need, I assure you.

JOSIE. You don't understand. People like me only get one chance.

DAI. Josie, please – please just let me... Can you listen, just for a moment?

JOSIE *looks up at him.*

These chats, these 'interviews', what we're checking for is... Are you a murderer, a child molester or a Conservative? That's pretty much it – that's the grounds for dismissal.

JOSIE (*sniffs*). What're you saying?

DAI. And you're not, are you?

JOSIE. No.

DAI. Didn't think so. You are a Party member, a union officer, you work in steel. Your family are good, honest people.

JOSIE. I'll tell Dad that.

DAI. Of course being a grocer's daughter, that does count against you in today's political climate.

JOSIE (*laughs*). Right.

DAI. Furthermore, you are an intelligent, passionate, colourful woman, who – not *colourful*, but... characterful – a woman of great character who would make a very fine council candidate indeed.

JOSIE. So you mean…?

DAI. So I mean you're not getting out of this that easy. You're one of us, anyone can see that. You'll go on our roster, then there's another shortlisting meeting before the member vote, but that should all be a formality.

JOSIE. Honestly?

DAI. Scout's honour. Councillor Two Soups, here we come.

Scene ends.

Scene Five

2018. VANESSA *and* IAN. VANESSA *is furious.*

VANESSA. Bastard.

IAN. Alright.

VANESSA. Pathetic, infantile –

IAN. Let's try to –

VANESSA. I mean this is, isn't it, this is just flinging toys out of the pram?

IAN. We all knew he was unhappy.

VANESSA. Unhappy? Yes, unhappy is… But can you believe the nerve of him?

IAN. I didn't think he'd go through with it, no.

VANESSA. But you knew what he was thinking?

IAN. He'd been running his mouth, but –

VANESSA. And it never crossed your mind to…? Because a little heads-up might've been, y'know, exactly within the remit of your job, actually, Ian.

IAN. And I apologise if –

VANESSA. That makes it all better then.

IAN. If I failed to take seriously –

VANESSA. Because actually what is the point of you, if not to keep the local wildlife under control?

IAN. Now I know it's not really me you're angry at, so –

VANESSA. I can be angry on multiple fronts. I can multitask.

IAN. Very good.

VANESSA. And you might hope that once – just once – that the Labour Party could be presented with an open goal and do something other than turn around and headbutt the referee.

IAN. 'Twas ever thus.

VANESSA. And people wonder why… (*Distracts herself.*) Oh, and just so you know, I am mad as all hell, but that was still a solid football analogy, so anyone who says I can't connect with the average male voter can go swivel.

IAN. Noted.

VANESSA. But seriously – Jerry Allen – former, yes, Party Treasurer – what else? Exec committee member, donor, fundraiser, union liaison. Now Jerry Allen wants to be Mayor? As an *independent*?! Can you believe him?

IAN. He has a lot of –

VANESSA. He was never… His name never came within a million miles of a shortlist, right? He was never in contention?

IAN. No.

VANESSA. He never even put himself forward?

IAN. Not that I'm aware of.

VANESSA. And now he pulls a stunt like this?

IAN. He… Jerry has been around forever. He has a very clear idea of how things should be done.

VANESSA. No women, no blacks, no Irish?

IAN. No – no I don't think that's fair –

VANESSA. He's a dinosaur.

IAN. He –

VANESSA. And he knows I'm the motherfucking asteroid.

IAN. He might be old-fashioned, but…

VANESSA (*reading*). 'In light of recent events we must concede that the Labour Party is no longer interested in representing the best interests of the working man. Therefore it is with a heavy heart – '

IAN. I've read it.

VANESSA. 'Heavy heart.' Three months from a cardiac arrest, more like.

IAN. Let's all take a breath –

VANESSA. I mean it. Slice him down the middle he bleeds coal tar and reconstituted pork.

IAN. Jerry has a base. He is known. He has something of a following.

VANESSA. Probably just caught in his gravitational pull, the fat fuck.

IAN. You need to take this a little seriously.

VANESSA. Do I look like I'm having fun?

IAN. He speaks to a certain type of demographically significant…

VANESSA. Professional Yorkshireman?

IAN. Man of the people. Business leader.

VANESSA. Leader?

IAN. Well respected as a –

VANESSA. He took his daddy's firm and he's running it into the ground. He's not some… some…

IAN. But the perception –

VANESSA. Right.

IAN. Close your eyes and picture the face of Labour in the Industrial North, you see Jerry Allen.

VANESSA. I try to close my eyes whenever I see Jerry Allen. I find it helps.

IAN. Seriously.

VANESSA. Right. Okay, right. Except he's screwed himself then, hasn't he? Because he's stabbing the Party in the back – he's tossed all that aside. Don't they have a word for that up here? A scab is what he is.

IAN. He wouldn't do this lightly.

VANESSA. But he has.

IAN. Exactly. Which is what scares me.

VANESSA. Yeah? Well I'm not afraid of him.

IAN. Scared because… You're right, this is a, a betrayal, if you like, a massive… And men like Jerry, whatever their faults, loyalty does matter to them. Labour men. Union men. Dyed-in-the-wool. So this is a big deal. It takes a lot to push a man like him that far.

VANESSA. And I'm really just that awful?

IAN. I don't want this to feel personal. But if he's a bellwether – if he's indicative of a larger problem – we have to take that on board.

VANESSA. Why doesn't he have to get on board with me?

IAN. Vanessa –

VANESSA. I mean it. I won! So why doesn't it feel like it?

IAN. You've not won anything yet.

VANESSA. That isn't true.

IAN. We're not home and dry. And my job, as your election officer, is to make sure we can finish what we started. You do understand that?

VANESSA. Yes. Yes, of course I do. (*Sighs, recomposes.*) Fine. So what does he want? Should I be sitting down with him? If I make him feel heard will he maybe shut up and go away?

IAN. No, no I think for now let's just... I think that could further antagonise... Sit tight. Leave it with me. I'll figure something out.

VANESSA. Right. Okay. Thank you.

Scene ends.

Scene Six

1988. DAI *and* JOSIE *are at a branch party meeting house.*

JOSIE. So... That just happened.

DAI. How do you feel?

JOSIE. Good. Yeah, I think good. Just...

DAI. A little anticlimactic?

JOSIE. No –

DAI. I'm afraid we don't really do tickertape parades up here, but...

JOSIE. Just quick – in and out before... Didn't get the chance to use my sock puppets or anything.

DAI (*laughs*). Good to hold something back. It's a big step, anyway – an important step. So – congratulations.

JOSIE. I haven't won anything yet.

DAI. *Au contraire.* You have secured your Party's nomination – that's the biggest hurdle around here. The rosette will do a lot of the heavy lifting now.

JOSIE. I'm not going to –

DAI. I know.

JOSIE. I'm doing this so I can do something, you know?

DAI. Absolutely – and you will. Without sock puppets – without soup – just you. I don't think they knew what'd hit them in there.

JOSIE. How do you mean?

DAI. I mean you... It's a good thing! You have a presence – an energy.

JOSIE. Yeah?

DAI. They'd never seen anything like you.

JOSIE. Yeah, well, maybe not.

DAI. Not like... I think people were excited – excited by the idea of you.

JOSIE. They didn't all look thrilled.

DAI. But they were all paying attention.

JOSIE. Maybe.

DAI. I should call Kenny at the... Have you met Kenny? And his wife Helen, who you'll love. Both just... Big movers and shakers – great people. She's a force of nature. Three kids, all terrific, never stops for breath.

JOSIE. Right.

DAI. Anyway, I'd love to introduce you.

JOSIE. Yeah, great – absolutely.

DAI. Because she – one of the things I thought you might... Helen's a housing officer by day, but actually her big thing is childcare provision.

JOSIE. Right.

DAI. Which is something none of us are taking seriously enough, actually – and I did think of you, because it's a real area where... If we want to create a family-friendly, a woman-friendly environment, then we have to ensure...

JOSIE. Uh-huh.

DAI. And she's just smashing – I think you'd have a lot to talk about.

JOSIE. Yeah. No, definitely. I mean I'm all for anyone who –

DAI. It's a good fit for you.

JOSIE. Yeah. (*Beat*.) But I mean you do know I don't?

DAI. Hmm?

JOSIE. Kids – you know I don't have any?

DAI. Right. Yes.

JOSIE. So I've no experience with –

DAI. And is that because of a lack of appropriate childcare provision in the workplace?

JOSIE. Um, I think it's more to do with not having a boyfriend, but –

DAI. Hah. Okay. Alright, and I didn't mean to… I'm not suggesting that just because you're a woman, but I think because you *are* a woman, I think you'll have certain insights, certain knowledge, certain areas –

JOSIE. Not really.

DAI. You'll campaign on a range of issues, naturally, but it's good to have a key… a focus – something you're known for.

JOSIE. Yeah. No, of course. I guess… I just sort of presumed it'd be steel.

DAI (*slightly surprised*). Steel?

JOSIE. Yeah. Maybe manufacturing in general, but –

DAI. Right.

JOSIE. It's what I do. It's what I know.

DAI. Yes. No of course.

JOSIE. Not… I mean I am only a junior, a very junior engineer, but in terms of expertise –

DAI. Yes. Now absolutely, now that is… All I would say is, when it comes to steel, I would tread a little carefully.

JOSIE. Why?

DAI. I would… Steel can… Steel has the potential to become a bit of an albatross, if I'm honest.

JOSIE. Right.

DAI. A bit of a dangerous thing to hitch your wagon to. I'm no expert, not like you, but I do sit in various rooms. I'm meant to give a talk, actually, to some business leaders next week on the future of industry beyond denationalisation. Do you want to hear what I've got so far?

JOSIE. Um, sure.

DAI (*clears throat*). 'There isn't one.'

JOSIE. Ah.

DAI. In layman's terms. Do you see what I'm saying?

JOSIE. Not really.

DAI. I'm saying don't shackle yourself to –

JOSIE. Because I don't – I don't accept that… There are challenges, yes, but opportunities too. It isn't hopeless.

DAI. Well, I am glad to hear that.

JOSIE. I mean it.

DAI. Good. In fact if you could elaborate on that for me before next Tuesday I'd be very grateful.

JOSIE. Sure. Yeah, definitely I can… Do you want to hear about this right now?

DAI. Please.

JOSIE. Right. No, it isn't all sunshine and roses, but… Okay. So first off, the technology – from an engineering side it's… The processes we're developing, they're safer, cleaner, more efficient, and that is –

DAI. Wonderful.

JOSIE. Yeah. Yes, it's great. So exciting. And also awful, but –

DAI. I'm sorry?

JOSIE. Great because it's impressive, it's a testament to everyone involved. And awful because right now progress means efficiency and that means man hours per tonne of steel produced, and, and yeah, as a mathematician – as an engineer – there's only one way those numbers are meant to go. And those numbers are better now. Business is numbers.

Science is numbers. I can give you numbers to pass on to people in suits that will show them we are in rude health.

DAI. I see.

JOSIE. But there are people too. There are people behind the numbers, and the more efficient, the more innovative, the better I do my job, the fewer people we get to employ. So I don't like to call that progress – not the progress we need.

DAI. Of course.

JOSIE. So what I would tell them – not to put words in your mouth, but if I was there – I'd tell them we can do better – think bigger, aim higher. I'd tell them we're not out of options. I'd tell them that progress doesn't look like just one thing.

DAI. Right. Thank you.

JOSIE. And let me... I will write you down some numbers, if that'd help.

DAI. That would be marvellous.

JOSIE. And I don't have to campaign on it – whatever's best politically, I'm not... But that is a battle I'll always be fighting, regardless of any... It's who we are – and numbers won't always tell you that. Men and women of steel. That's always going to mean something.

Scene ends.

Scene Seven

2018. VANESSA *and* IAN. *They are discussing a document* IAN *has prepared.*

VANESSA. Steel?

IAN. Trust me.

VANESSA. Seriously?

IAN. Still means quite a lot up here.

VANESSA. Yes, I am aware, but –

IAN. Steel is a vote-winner.

VANESSA. Now look – industry, yes – commitment to industry, manufacturing, advanced technologies, all kinds of –

IAN. Isn't enough.

VANESSA. I am proposing radical investment in infrastructure, retraining schemes, in high-tech, ecologically sound... But this? (*Quoting from a document.*) 'To plot our brightest future we must look back to our greatest triumphs.'

IAN. Objections?

VANESSA. If your greatest triumph was during the Industrial Revolution you might need to move on.

IAN. Steel isn't just a trade, it's an identity.

VANESSA. Tell me about it.

IAN. And it's one you need.

VANESSA. I'm not going to pledge millions to prop up a dying industry because it makes people feel warm and fuzzy inside.

IAN. Steel is what gets Jerry Allen off our backs.

VANESSA. He's not a serious –

IAN. He is. He is your only serious competition. And his main line – the *only* line of attack he needs – is that you're out of touch, an outsider. You don't know what matters to us up here.

VANESSA. Wouldn't it be cheaper just to do a photo-op with a Yorkshire pudding or something?

IAN. It wouldn't have worked against Debbie – she's as local as they come. Even Carol it wouldn't have stuck on, because she's got the business background. This is where you're vulnerable.

VANESSA. But steel isn't… Trust me on this – I do actually know what I'm talking about – steel, without getting too technical, actually just sucks.

IAN. It sucks?

VANESSA. It honestly does. Against all environmental, socio-economic and human-centric metrics, the steel industry as it exists today sucks balls. Didn't always, but does now. It doesn't need another rescue package, it needs putting out of its misery.

IAN. And this is why we have a problem.

VANESSA. On emissions, on working conditions, on financial viability, there are so many better… Why are we even pursuing this?

IAN. And until you can answer that you'll never win here.

VANESSA. Are you a cat person?

IAN. Excuse me?

VANESSA. Or a pet person in general? I doubt it – people with pets really like to tell you about their pets, so… Anyway, the problem with pet-people is they get attached, they form these emotional bonds completely disproportionate to the reality of the situation – are you with me?

IAN. Not entirely.

VANESSA. My mum – she was a cat person, big time – before she got sick. Now she can't really… She adopted this mangy old stray after I moved out – knackered from day one – and then he got some… I don't know, some growth, needed operating, and it was going to cost her five grand. Five thousand pounds! And that isn't – that's not money they just had lying around. Five grand for what was going to extend his life by another six months – a year, tops. But she insisted, so Dad forked out for it.

IAN. And you would've drowned it in the canal?

VANESSA. I very sensitively, very humanely I suggested –

IAN. Classic sign of a psychopath, that.

VANESSA. I wasn't volunteering to do it myself!

IAN. Are you sure you're not a Tory?

VANESSA. My point is the logical thing – any rational person would conclude –

IAN. Just get another cat?

VANESSA. Yes! Exactly! Get another cat, or a goldfish, or a hobby. Cut your losses – move on.

IAN. Easy as that.

VANESSA. No, it's not easy – it's hard, and it's heartbreaking. She really loved that cat, even when its fur was falling out and it started pissing on the carpets. But it wasn't healthy – sometimes only an outsider can see that.

IAN. We are not in a toxic relationship with steel.

VANESSA. You're not even in the relationship any more. They're gone! You need to put yourself back out there! And that's scary – it is – it's terrifying – but you deserve better. The people aren't crying out for steel jobs, they're just crying out for *something*, and this – (*Waving document.*) This is unworthy of them. This is Jerry Allen, promising more of the shitty same because he lacks the imagination to offer anything new. Screw that. This isn't a pit town. It's not some little hamlet in the arse-end of nowhere with one road in and one road out. There are options. And we need more options and better options, yes, but that's what we should be investing our energy in. The truth that dare not speak its name isn't that the steel industry is doomed, it's that it's actually fine that it is.

IAN. Do you actually want to win this?

VANESSA. We are going to win.

IAN. Not if you ever say anything like that again.

VANESSA. Ian, come on –

IAN. No. No, you will hear me. I'm not here to tell you what to do once you're in office, I'm just trying to drag you over the finish line. You need this. You need something, because we are taking on water fast and this is the best way I know how to bail you out. Please. Listen to me.

VANESSA. Wow. Now you're actually scaring me a little.

IAN. Good. Get scared, learn the numbers, sell it hard. Don't blow it.

Scene ends.

Scene Eight

A split timeline. DAI, *in 1988, and* VANESSA, *in 2018, are both making speeches at Cutler's Hall.*

DAI. Master Cutler –

VANESSA. Ladies and gentlemen –

DAI. Distinguished guests –

VANESSA. Friends –

DAI. Brothers –

VANESSA. Comrades.

DAI. These are uncertain times.

VANESSA. This is an age of innovation.

DAI. There are worries. There are fears.

VANESSA. There are challenges, yes, but opportunities as well.

DAI. There is the suggestion in some parts that what we do – who we are – the very essence of our being is under threat. That perhaps we are already far too late – the damage has been done – that there is no way back from here.

VANESSA. The Labour Party has a plan – a plan that will leave no citizen behind.

DAI. But if there is no way back, then let there be no doubt that we shall be offering an alternative way forward.

VANESSA. And we in Labour are continuing to do what we have always done. To defend the rights of the many. To strengthen communities. To provide opportunity – opportunity for all – opportunity for anyone who will grasp it. Master Cutler, I say to you that the purpose of government – the purpose of the Labour Party – is to make spoons. We make spoons for the simple reason that people need to eat, and we must ensure everyone has the means to. Conservative governments see things differently. They say, 'Well, everyone I know has a spoon already – they've got drawers full of them. This fellow here, he was actually *born* with a very nice spoon just sitting there right in his mouth. Why should I spend my money making something that all of *my* friends have already?' They will tell you that the people are not really hungry, they are simply lazy. They will look to their full plates and not believe anybody's cupboards could be bare.

But I'm not talking about free lunches. The Labour Party doesn't want – has never been in the business of handouts. All we want to do is make sure everybody has a spoon – we want to make sure everybody has the tools they need to feed themselves. Making spoons – that's what I got into government for. And not silver spoons – spoons of solid steel! As your Metro Mayor I'm going to make sure we're right back in the business of making things, and that there is a spine of steel in everything we do.

DAI*'s closing speech is altogether a bit more rousing and successful than* VANESSA*'s.*

DAI. Now this, my friends, is what I call on you to do. I call on you to be brave. I call on you to be resolute. I call on you to hold your nerve, and honour all of those who came before us. To look to the example they set. To build upon their legacy. At times like this it falls upon us all to be Men of Steel. For we are stronger than we know. For our faith shall be unwavering. For that steel is not just something we make

– that our fathers made, and their fathers before them – it is something inside of us. Something at our core. We are – yes, we are – those things we forged. We poured our molten selves into each mould, tempered the metal with the sweat from our brows, kept the furnace blazing with our very breath – but our lives do not begin and end at the factory gates. We are not defined by this, and this alone. And we'll fight – we shall fight – to keep those jobs – to keep those gates open – to keep making those things of strength and beauty that have made us the envy of the world. But whatever happens, whatever fate our future holds, we shall always be Men of Steel. That can never be taken from us. That can never be cast into doubt. Men of Steel, who shall not be downtrodden. Men of Steel, who shall not be overlooked, or cast aside. Men of Steel, who cannot be forgotten, forsaken, humbled or humiliated, because we were made too well for that. We are Men of Steel, and we shall never lose our shine!

End of Act One.

ACT TWO

Scene One

Split scene. DAI *and* VANESSA *are both reading newspaper accounts of their recent speeches.* DAI *holds an actual newspaper,* VANESSA *perhaps consults a tablet.*

DAI. 'All hail the Steel Caesar'.

VANESSA. 'Make way for the Steel Lady'.

DAI (*calling over his shoulder, off stage*). You read this?

VANESSA (*to herself*). Jesus Christ.

DAI (*continues reading*). 'The city's very own Welsh Windbag, councillor Dai Griffiths, made a barnstorming speech to Party faithful last night, but anyone hoping the council would be adopting a less severe – or even less insane – stance were bound to be disappointed.'

He chuckles.

VANESSA. 'Miss Gallacher, with her cropped curls and plunging silk blouse cut an…' Oh, for crying out… 'cut an *exotic* figure at Cutler's Hall…'

DAI (*still calling off*). Excelled themselves this time.

VANESSA. 'The outfit said "Hello Boys", and she intended to seduce. "I'm one of you," she pleaded, though many will still need convincing.'

DAI. 'Perhaps the hills are to blame (seven, just like Rome, the locals never tire of telling you); the thinner air causing Mr Griffiths to lose all his senses…'

VANESSA. 'For all the predictable Tory-bashing and lip service to local industry, this was not a typical call to arms. But then Miss Gallacher is not your typical Labour candidate. With her…' Christ Almighty. 'Her lavish praise of public-private partnerships and a stern pledge to help people help themselves, the tone was more Mrs T than TUC.'

DAI. 'Whatever the source of his lunacy, this Steel Caesar of the People's Republic took great pleasure in laying out his stall.'

VANESSA (*calling off*). Can you believe them?

DAI (*also calling off*). You getting all this?

1988. A shift in light, as VANESSA *now becomes* JOSIE, *jumping into* DAI*'s timeline.*

JOSIE. How're you feeling?

DAI. I've been called some pretty spectacular things before, but –

JOSIE. Yeah. Although –

DAI. Your handiwork, is this.

JOSIE. I only –

DAI. Your masterpiece.

JOSIE. I... You did ask for... Not that I'm, I didn't, I wasn't –

DAI. Relax.

JOSIE. I didn't realise you were going to use quite so much of what I gave you, if I'm honest.

DAI. Why wouldn't I? It was all magnificent. (*Chuckles*.) The Steel Caesar!

JOSIE. So you're... you're happy with – ?

DAI. Don't you think I'm suitably imperial?

JOSIE. No, of course. I just –

DAI. I mean Caesar is... He's one of the greats, isn't he? The greatest, arguably. Not one of the... like the... the horse one?

JOSIE. The horse one?

DAI. The mad one. Y'know – horses – violins.

JOSIE. Violins? Oh... Nero? Fiddled while –

DAI. Right. Yes. Fiddled with horses while Rome burned.

JOSIE *giggles*.

But seriously – seriously though – schoolboy error. Who uses Caesar as an insult? Who thinks being Caesar is a bad thing?

JOSIE. Brutus?

DAI. Alright, smart alec, but – but the point is – they're calling me an emperor. They're giving me power – status – this shows I'm under their skin.

JOSIE. Right.

DAI. Nicest thing they've ever said about me. Steel Caesar, it just sounds… Trips off the… It isn't… I don't know – Pig Iron Napoleon –

JOSIE (*laughs*). Sure.

DAI. Or… Mineshaft Mussolini.

JOSIE. Flat-cap Castro?

DAI. Oh, I don't know – I quite like that actually.

JOSIE. Because on the… I did worry 'Men of Steel' could sound a little – read as Stalinist, but –

DAI. Superman, isn't it?

JOSIE. Which is why I suggested… 'men and women of steel' – it's a bit softer, more inclusive, not as –

DAI. Yes. I mean yes, but it hardly scans.

JOSIE. Right.

DAI. As a piece of oratory.

JOSIE. Hmm.

DAI. And 'men' isn't… Just universal, isn't it? 'Friends, Romans, countrymen.' As in 'mankind' – not excluding –

JOSIE. No.

DAI (*still grinning*). No, it was perfect – pretty perfect, I'd say. I do feel bad for you, actually, but we'll find you something else.

JOSIE. Sorry?

DAI. Other than steel – for you to campaign on. We really must now. A bit of steel, certainly, because they're lapping this up, but you need your own voice, not just parroting…

JOSIE. Right.

DAI. And that sounds horribly unfair, I know, but you understand?

JOSIE. I… Yeah. I mean we're all on the same team, aren't we?

DAI. Absolutely. Yes, absolutely that. 'Steel Caesar'! Hah. Can't get over it. Get them to call you steel anything up here and it's a home run.

Lights shift and we're in 2018, JOSIE *and* DAI *immediately becoming* VANESSA *and* IAN. *The article is still being discussed.*

VANESSA. 'The Steel Lady'?

IAN. Try not to –

VANESSA. 'Close your eyes and you'd swear the city had found its own self-styled Steel Lady.'

IAN. Ignore it. Don't rise to it.

VANESSA. Ignore it?

IAN. It's trash. It's a gossip blog.

VANESSA. 'Self-styled', as if I've intentionally, actively modelled myself on… I feel sick – actually physically sick –

IAN. If you look at it from a… 'Steel Lady' – 'Woman of Steel' – same thing –

VANESSA. They are not the same thing!

IAN. In so many words –

VANESSA. 'Woman of Steel' gets a statue – 'Steel Lady' gets an… an effigy.

IAN. It's what we wanted. Steel is good. Steel ticks boxes.

VANESSA. Come on!

IAN. Strong, tough, local – everything we planned –

VANESSA. And that's honestly what you think they're implying, is it?

IAN. Doesn't matter. We lean into it – take ownership of –

VANESSA. Uh-huh. And I don't look like an idiot at all in that scenario, do I?

IAN. I'm not sure I follow.

VANESSA. 'Oh, Steel Lady – thank you very much. You love a bit of steel up here, don't you? How welcoming! What an honour!' Entirely oblivious to any of the… No, because I'm just another airhead millennial with no sense of history – file Thatcher alongside the Spice Girls under hashtag-feminism hashtag-boss-bitch culturally tone-deaf bullshit –

IAN. Yes, alright. Fair point.

VANESSA. Too stupid to even know when I'm being insulted. No, must be a compliment – couldn't possibly still be upset about Maggie round here, could they? Not after all this time. Well tell me, Ian – do you reckon there might be one or two who still hold a grudge?

IAN. I dare say.

VANESSA. So if we could try really quite hard to avoid 'leaning in' to any comparison between… (*Glancing down at the article*.) I mean, for fuck's sake – they even gave me her hair – they photoshopped it.

IAN. Didn't see that.

VANESSA. That's 'self-styled', is it? It's slander – I should sue for defamation.

IAN. Alright, just –

VANESSA. But then I can't – I can't actually call them out on it either, can I? I can't say 'Steel Lady – how dare you?' Because then I'm insulting steel – I'm too good for steel. Like I've told them to go shove their Bessemer converter where the sun don't shine.

IAN. Bessemer converter?

VANESSA. I told you I know my stuff.

IAN. I'm impressed.

VANESSA. I told you I didn't want to get drawn into... Well screw them. It's pathetic, it's cheap, it's beneath me, and you know what, I won't engage with it. We don't give them the satisfaction. No comment. How's that for steel?

Scene ends.

Scene Two

1988. DAI *is visiting* JOSIE. *She isn't well.*

DAI. I brought you soup.

JOSIE. Dai –

DAI. Don't worry, Margie made it, not me.

JOSIE. She didn't have to.

DAI. I did suggest it might trigger a flashback, but she insisted. Chicken and leek – highly restorative.

JOSIE. I'm fine.

DAI. You're not.

JOSIE. Honestly –

DAI. She's on quite the health kick. I bear the brunt of it. She said to me, she said, 'Dai, if you are going to insist on calling yourself Caesar you might try a salad once in a while.'

JOSIE *smiles.*

That's better. Now, I've also come for a serious word in your ear.

JOSIE. What? What's happened?

DAI. Consider this your official cease and desist order.

JOSIE. I'm not –

DAI. You're meant to be on bed rest.

JOSIE. I am.

DAI. I have it on good authority that in the past twenty-four hours you've called Andy Yates at Highways and Byways, Roger at the NUM, Gareth in Town Planning said you'd phoned three times –

JOSIE. And I phoned them all from my bed.

DAI. You don't need to be doing any of this. You're running a fever and you're still campaigning twice as hard as any councillor in the city – ten times harder than most. You can slow down a little.

JOSIE. It's just a bit of cold.

DAI. Bill held this seat for twenty years and I never saw him do so much as give out a flyer.

JOSIE. I'm not Bill.

DAI. Which is only a good thing, as far as I'm concerned.

JOSIE. And you're not everyone.

DAI. Can you not...? I know you're a worrier, but please believe me when I say you are every inch the attractive candidate. Not right this moment, I'll concede – I prefer you without the phlegm.

JOSIE. You don't see what I see – you don't notice it.

DAI. Josie –

JOSIE. I can't take anything for granted.

DAI. Speaking from experience –

JOSIE. You don't have experience of this. You don't have to fight like I do. Please.

DAI. And if you collapse with nervous exhaustion before election night, what was the point of any of this?

JOSIE. I told you I'm fine.

DAI. Then at least try to… Preserve your energy. Focus your approach. Helen said you had a good chat about childcare.

JOSIE. Yeah. You're right – she's brilliant.

DAI. I knew you'd hit it off. And that's enough – more than enough for now.

JOSIE. But I still don't know anything about it. I'm not –

DAI. You're a fast learner – you'll be an expert in no time.

JOSIE. Yeah, but –

DAI. No buts. Now, I've been given reheating instructions that even I can follow, so – point me towards your kitchen please.

JOSIE. Okay. It's this way.

Scene ends. Snap to:

Scene Three

2018. VANESSA *and* IAN. IAN *is reading from a document.*

IAN. 'The industry must face certain harsh realities – '

VANESSA. I know what it says.

IAN. 'We believe there is no long-term, financially viable future in – '

VANESSA. I know because I wrote it.

IAN. Quite.

VANESSA. Not… Not all of it, but –

IAN. But enough.

VANESSA. I told you I'd done my research.

IAN. You didn't tell me about this.

VANESSA. These aren't personal opinions. These are the objective findings and recommendations of a politically neutral working group looking into the long-term future of manufacturing.

IAN. Which state the steel industry should be quietly left to die.

VANESSA. Which suggest there are better options –

IAN. Like your mum's mangy old cat.

VANESSA. If you like, yes.

IAN. Do you realise what a complete fucking disaster this is?

VANESSA. I've got some idea, yeah.

IAN. It's not just the… It isn't just this – I mean this is bad enough – this is really pretty bad just by itself –

VANESSA. It isn't –

IAN. But – and just let me… But it's the… You can't write a paper – co-author a paper saying close the factory gates and then turn around and declare yourself the Steel Lady. You just can't!

VANESSA. Which is what I told you! I told you I didn't want to get into steel. I told you there was no future in it. My views haven't changed.

IAN. You stood up, you laid out, you… you and your spoons –

VANESSA. You made me!

IAN. Oh please.

VANESSA. Oh please what?

IAN. Since when has anyone been capable of making Vanessa Gallacher do or say anything she didn't want to?

VANESSA. You insisted, you… I was explicit, I was clear, I was consistent. Industry yes, investment yes, but don't… And you, you said that wasn't good enough. You said just tell them what they want to hear. I warned you –

IAN (*waving the document*). And I didn't know this was out there!

VANESSA. Sure. Except it's kind of your job to know, isn't it?

IAN. If a candidate won't divulge, deliberately conceals –

VANESSA. I never –

IAN. I'm not taking the fall for this. I've been putting out fires for you since day one, but *this*.

VANESSA. If people actually read it – the detail of it – they'd understand… We make a series of recommendations, none of which are –

IAN. 'Labour Mayor declares war on steel.'

VANESSA. That isn't true – it doesn't say –

IAN. This is the… It epitomises the flip-flopping, the opportunism, the hypocrisy of… And why it's perfect, why it's so deadly – is it's the scandal everyone *wants* to believe. Like the pig-fucking – you could just picture it. They look at you, Vanessa, and they think, 'Yeah, yeah, that's her down to a tee. We knew she was never one of us.'

VANESSA. Don't say that.

IAN. Jerry's lot are going to have a field day: Titan of Industry versus the woman who'd sell us for scrap.

VANESSA. So what do we do?

IAN. Now she's asking.

VANESSA. I'm asking for your help, yes.

IAN. Is there more to come?

VANESSA. Sorry?

IAN. Is there any more to…? Have you drowned any puppies lately? Are you carrying Michael Gove's love child?

VANESSA. I… There is nothing else pertinent that I'm aware of, no.

IAN. Right, well let's hope not.

VANESSA. This isn't… I mean, no one's died.

IAN. Not yet.

VANESSA. I haven't done anything wrong. All I did was...
This is going to be fine. Ian? This is going to be fine, isn't it?

He doesn't immediately answer. Scene ends.

Scene Four

1988. DAI *waits in a long overcoat and scarf, holding a bundle of flyers.* JOSIE *enters, in a rush. She's a bit shaky and trying to hide it.*

JOSIE. Sorry, sorry.

DAI. Don't worry.

JOSIE. You must be frozen.

DAI. I'm layered up. And you – are you okay to be out?

JOSIE. Yeah, I'm good. Much better.

They start talking together.

DAI. / So I thought we could –

JOSIE. It's just my parents, they had a –

DAI. Sorry.

JOSIE. No, sorry, go on.

DAI. Your parents?

JOSIE. Doesn't matter. We can just get going.

DAI. Are they alright?

JOSIE. Yeah. Yeah, I just... I had to go over this morning. But they're fine – they're both fine.

DAI. Good.

JOSIE. Yeah. Honestly.

DAI. Are you sure?

JOSIE. They had a… No, they are, but… Sorry. It's nothing.
Someone smashed one of the shop windows last night.

DAI. Oh.

JOSIE. Yeah.

DAI. Right.

JOSIE. And, y'know, because they live above… Because their
flat is –

DAI. But they're…? They weren't – ?

JOSIE. No, they're both okay. Mum slept through it, so –

DAI. And did they take much?

JOSIE. No. No, they didn't take anything, I don't think.

DAI. Oh. (*Beat.*) Well good. That's good, isn't it?

JOSIE. Um, yeah.

DAI. I wonder why? Do you think they were scared off, or – ?

JOSIE. Um, no. No, I don't think they wanted to… They put
a brick, uh, through the window. They weren't trying to
break in, they just wanted to… to…

DAI. Ah.

JOSIE. To do whatever these people want to do when they…
Shit. Sorry.

DAI. I see. (*Beat.*) And you think, you think this was a…?

JOSIE. 'Go Home.' There was a note, um, tied to the brick. Said
'Go home'.

DAI. Right.

JOSIE. Fairly unambiguous, really.

DAI. Jesus.

JOSIE. Not really a lot of… of…

DAI. Are you okay? What can I – ?

JOSIE. And what I kept on thinking, I mean beyond the, the, the
shaking rage and the general… They live there. Mum and
Dad – they literally live above the shop.

DAI. Must have been terrifying.

JOSIE. No, but I mean… They're right there. And you're
saying 'go home' – they were home. He was in bed. So what
you've made him do, what you've done is you've got him
up, you've marched him downstairs to, to, to pick up broken
glass on his hands and knees and then find this note, this
scrawled, stupid, childish… He was home.

DAI. I don't have words, honestly.

JOSIE. No.

DAI. Have they spoken to the police?

JOSIE. Yeah. They came while I was there. They were fine –
nice – took it as seriously as you'd hope.

DAI. Good.

JOSIE. But they're not… Most likely just an isolated incident,
they said. They did have one other, but that was – I was still
in school – must've been twenty years ago.

DAI. One other…?

JOSIE. Another window put out, yeah.

DAI. Right.

JOSIE. But y'know, two in twenty years, I mean that's… Not
too bad going, is it?

DAI. I would say once is far too much.

JOSIE. Yeah. Of course yeah, but –

DAI. But they're not being targeted.

JOSIE. No. My dad, he's… Well, you've met him. Difficult
man to dislike.

DAI. Yes.

JOSIE. And we always say he worries too much about getting
people to like him, but… The officer – one of the officers –
he asked to see the note – the 'go home' note – and Dad went
dead funny. Said he didn't see why they needed it, then he
doesn't know where it is, then he thinks he threw it away,

and we can all tell he's lying, so I say, 'Dad, what's the matter? What's going on?' and the police, they're nice, but they're insistent, and they're starting to get suspicious now, and eventually, eventually he throws his hands up and he says, 'Alright, fine, fine, just don't overreact,' and he fetches it, and I understand now, because it's not just any scrap of paper, it's written on one of these. (*Pulls out a crumpled flyer.*) 'Josie Kirkwood: Your New Councillor.'

Pause.

'Josie Kirkwood: Go Home.'

DAI. Oh. That is… That is just…

JOSIE. So you're right – no one's targeting them. No, it's me.

DAI. Josie –

JOSIE. And all they ever wanted for me – a good man, couple of kids, a quiet, respectable… Couldn't give them any of that – only this.

DAI. This isn't your doing.

JOSIE. That's my face.

DAI. You cannot be / held –

JOSIE. Which I never wanted printed on anything, but…

DAI. The police, they, they… They're going to find whoever… And I won't allow… I will do everything I can to make sure –

JOSIE. Is this just…? Is this how it's going to be now?

DAI. Of course not.

JOSIE. Because I thought… And no disrespect, but who cares this much about the council? This isn't high profile – it's not drinks with the ambassador and a cover spread for *Smash Hits*, it's boring, behind-the-scenes anonymity.

DAI. Generally speaking, yes.

JOSIE. It isn't painting a target on your back. It isn't bricks through my parents' windows. I didn't sign up for that.

DAI. No.

JOSIE. If that's what comes with the job then…

DAI. It isn't. I promise you, this isn't… (*Gesturing to the wodge of flyers he's still holding*.) Look, we will resolve it, but let's forget about this for today. Let me buy you breakfast.

JOSIE. I'll be okay.

DAI. I know you will. Come on – cup of tea, at least – fuel of empires.

JOSIE. I'll be… I just…

DAI. Something warm and you'll be right as rain. But what I won't – what I can't allow – we will not be intimidated. We will not be ruled by fear, or dictated to by the pea-brained troglodytes who represent the lowest – the absolute dregs of our society. The actions of imbeciles shall not keep the world from knowing Josie Kirkwood.

JOSIE. Why're you so nice to me?

DAI. Because you are the future, and I'd like to stay on the right side of you. Come on.

JOSIE. No.

DAI. Excuse me?

JOSIE. We give out half of these, then we stop for tea.

DAI. Josie –

JOSIE. We plough on. I'm not going to hide behind the rosette. If I'm asking for their vote they should know who I am.

DAI. If you're sure.

JOSIE. I'm sure. We're on the home stretch. Josie Kirkwood's coming home.

Scene ends.

Scene Five

2018. VANESSA *is just finishing a campaign speech.*

VANESSA. Because we deserve better. Better than we've been given, better than we've been promised, better than we've grown accustomed to. I don't just want to build houses, I want castles. We won't just bring jobs, but vocations. I won't just be your mayor, I will be a citizen, working beside you day after day to bring you the future you truly deserve. Thank you.

Slightly lukewarm applause. As VANESSA *steps off,* IAN *is waiting. Their opening exchanges are a bit stilted, like they're still slightly tiptoeing around each other.*

Okay?

IAN. Oh. Yes, yes, very…

VANESSA. Nice crowd – good turnout – thanks for that.

IAN. I do my best.

VANESSA. I'm not sure about 'castles' – bit grandiose, maybe? A bit Marie Antoinette.

IAN. Oh?

VANESSA. Yeah, a bit… 'The peasants have no affordable housing' – 'Then let them live in castles!'

IAN. I see. (*Beat.*) I'm not sure it's a reference many will be leaping to, but…

VANESSA. No.

IAN. But we can –

VANESSA. I'm probably just second-guessing myself.

IAN. Tweak it if you want to.

VANESSA. Yeah. (*Beat.*) Are you alright? Is everything – ?

IAN. Can I have a word?

VANESSA. Aren't we already?

IAN. Yes. Sorry. Yes.

VANESSA. What is it?

IAN. It's...

> IAN *glances around and they move slightly to one side, as if stepping out of anyone's earshot.*

VANESSA. What's the matter?

IAN. I asked you if there was anything else.

VANESSA. What're you talking about?

IAN. Vanessa –

VANESSA. What?

IAN. Simon Mullaney.

VANESSA (*after a pause*). What about him?

IAN. You know him?

VANESSA. Would you be asking if I didn't?

IAN. Professor Simon Mullaney was the most frequently cited expert in your paper on –

VANESSA. Again, it wasn't *my* paper, I was part / of a –

IAN. Part of a working group, yes. And the testimony of Simon Mullaney formed a significant part of your findings.

VANESSA. In certain areas, yes.

IAN. Certain key areas.

VANESSA. Maybe. What is – ?

IAN. And he was your boyfriend at the time?

VANESSA. No.

IAN. No?

VANESSA. No. He was never really... Our thing was... It wasn't a... But whatever it was it was over long before –

IAN. But you brought him in – that was you?

VANESSA. Yes.

IAN. And he was paid a fee?

VANESSA. I'm sure he was. As he should've been.

IAN. I see.

VANESSA. He was a relevant, highly respected expert working
    in –

IAN (*quoting from a document*). 'Climate Scientist attempts
    citizen's arrest on Russian oil baron.'

VANESSA. That was… That's an entirely separate issue. That
    wasn't –

IAN. 'Loopy Prof in hot water over Thames stunt.'

VANESSA. Again, separate. And misleading. He only –

IAN. 'How shedding my shoes helped me bare my soul.'
    Professor Simon Mullaney. That was for the *Guardian*,
    believe it or not.

VANESSA. What's your point?

IAN. Something of a character, would you say?

VANESSA. Simon is a brilliant man with a lot of strongly held
    beliefs, but he is rigorous and scientific, and… and all his
    findings, all his recommendations on the work we did
    together were –

IAN. Jesus!

VANESSA. Were uncontroversial, were fastidiously –

IAN. Are you starting to understand just how unequivocally
    fucked you are?

VANESSA. No! No, I'm not actually.

IAN. Right.

VANESSA. How is this…? How have I behaved…? I was
    invited on to a working group, we looked at the evidence
    presented to us, we spoke to relevant experts, we made our
    recommendations.

IAN. And those expert recommendations – terrible
    recommendations – politically terrible, regardless of any…

They just happened to come from some barefoot mad-haired eco-anarchist who you were carrying on with.

VANESSA. He is a professor of environmental science.

IAN. Right.

VANESSA. Who I... I briefly, long before... And it wasn't 'carrying on', it was a... a...

IAN. Yes?

VANESSA. We didn't want to put a label on it, but...

IAN *rolls his eyes*.

But it was an adult, consensual –

IAN. Good.

VANESSA. I'm not ashamed of it. It wasn't sordid or coercive or in any way... We weren't picking out wedding china, but it was still a... a relationship, of sorts, that was entirely –

IAN. A polyamorous relationship? (*Beat.*) That is the term, isn't it? Polyamory? That is right?

VANESSA. Fuck off, Ian.

IAN. I'm not... I understand the London dating scene is very...

VANESSA. It was a... Why am I having this conversation with you?

IAN. Because you failed to have it with anyone else back when you should've.

VANESSA. We were each other's primary partners. He would also see other people, I did not. I ended the relationship – or whatever the fuck it was – eventually, because it turns out that I'm all for free love on paper but in practice it does my head in. Are you happy now?

IAN (*deadpan*). Ecstatic.

VANESSA. None of this should matter.

IAN. Jerry Allen is a family man.

VANESSA. Jerry Allen has pinched the arse of every female
    Labour Party volunteer this side of the Rother Valley, so
    let's not –

IAN. And unless you can prove that, you'd be wise not to
    repeat it.

VANESSA. Fuck! This is… Fuck! Who else has this?

IAN. Don't know.

VANESSA. Great.

IAN. But I found it, and I'm hardly Benedict What's-his-face.

VANESSA. Right.

IAN. If Jerry doesn't yet, we can assume it's only a matter of
    time.

VANESSA. Right. Okay then, right. Well that is… Okay, yes,
    not ideal – I see that. So. So, we… How should we do this?
    Should I talk to Simon? We should warn him if… And what
    about Party HQ? Do we make our own plan first, or…?

IAN. Some quiet words have been had already.

VANESSA. Oh. Oh right.

IAN. Nothing – not keeping you out of the loop –

VANESSA. No.

IAN. But just the speed that these things –

VANESSA. Yeah, sure. (*Beat.*) Okay. Well go on then.

IAN. Right. Well look, this isn't… There's a feeling… This is a
    must-win race for us – for everyone, here to Westminster –

VANESSA. Agreed.

IAN. And it was a can't-lose, but –

VANESSA. I still / think –

IAN. But it really – no – we really can't say that any more. And
    that isn't… Bottom line, a loss is unacceptable – can't
    happen – can't be allowed – so we all have to do whatever it
    takes to ensure against that.

VANESSA. Absolutely.

IAN. For the Party. Above all else.

VANESSA. Right.

IAN. You understand that's everyone's priority.

VANESSA. Great.

IAN. Good. And if we're honest, this was never the best fit for you, was it?

VANESSA. I'm sorry?

IAN. You tried – I know more than anyone, you bent over backwards, but –

VANESSA. What're you saying?

IAN. The consensus is… perhaps your candidacy has run its course.

Pause.

VANESSA (*laughs*). Are you serious?

IAN. I'm sorry.

VANESSA. You want me to stand down?

IAN. We think –

VANESSA. Because I fucked some guy who makes his own yogurt?

IAN. Not just because of that.

VANESSA. We are weeks away – literally weeks.

IAN. There's a… Obviously time is a factor, yes, but –

VANESSA. Jesus. Fucking Jesus.

IAN. The bigger picture is –

VANESSA. You're throwing me to the wolves?

IAN. No – absolutely not. Everyone wants to make sure you're looked after.

VANESSA. Sure. Right. Sure.

IAN. We will –

VANESSA. After I've been chased out with pitchforks?

IAN. We can protect you. We think so long as you're not the candidate here this needn't come out at all.

VANESSA. No. No, no, no, this is… No. This is crazy. This is… Forget me for a second, this would look terrible – this would make us all look –

IAN. Not if we give the right reason.

VANESSA. And what reason is that? (*Pause.*) Go on.

IAN. We were… I thought, potentially… And I'm not…

VANESSA. Spit it out.

IAN. I thought your mother.

VANESSA. Right.

IAN. I know that sounds –

VANESSA. No, very good.

IAN. People would –

VANESSA. Hmm. Good old early-onset dementia, it's got to be useful for something.

IAN. I'm sorry.

VANESSA. For what? The decaying of my mother's neural pathways or my political career?

IAN. I am personally, deeply very… Whatever our, um, differences –

VANESSA. This is bullshit! You must see that.

IAN. I've been promised – I asked, and they are fully… If you bow out gracefully they will absolutely find you something else.

VANESSA. Right.

IAN. You're young. General Election's only four years away – maybe much sooner – who knows?

VANESSA. Hah! Sure.

IAN. I've been given assurances –

VANESSA. That is just… Of all the… No! No, this is it! This is
the final… I make a success of this or I am over – through –
done – no more second chances.

IAN. You'd be surprised.

VANESSA. Not for someone like me.

IAN. No –

VANESSA. Yes! Two years – that was all I had as an MP – two
sorry years in a seat nobody thought I'd ever win in the first
place. No support. No resources. And do you know what I lost
it by? Do you?

IAN. No.

VANESSA. A hundred and twenty-seven votes. One hundred
and twenty-seven! I've been to weddings with bigger
congregations than that motherfucker's majority.

IAN. Like you say, it was a tough gig. You exceeded
everyone's –

VANESSA. No, but nonetheless – Vanessa Gallacher – former
MP – unseated before I'd even got the seat warm. This was
my redemption arc – my one shot.

IAN. You'll be looked after.

VANESSA. You think?

IAN. We do look after our own.

VANESSA. Of course you do. Yeah, I don't doubt that.

IAN. This is best for you too. Home or no home, you don't fit
here. Stick it out and they will paint you as out-of-touch,
parachuted-in, liberal metropolitan elite with your blue-sky
whatevers and your open relationships and your fundamental
lack of understanding for everything that makes this city great.

VANESSA. They tried that already.

IAN. Vanessa, please –

VANESSA. They can't do this! How would they even do this? If I were to – *if* – there'd be a, a what, some kind of…?

IAN. There'd be a fast-tracked selection process.

VANESSA. Right.

IAN. Local Campaign Forum would make a shortlist. Might not be time for a full member vote, but all above board and as transparent as time allows.

VANESSA. Naturally.

IAN. Of course everyone's very keen we should all get on the same page as soon as possible, time being of the essence.

VANESSA. Yes. Yes, of course.

Pause.

IAN. So – ?

VANESSA. So? So what? Jesus Ian, just give me a… I do apologise if I can't commit hari-kari in the time it takes to boil a kettle. So just –

IAN. Yes. Sorry. Yes.

VANESSA. Jesus. I'm tired. You know what, mostly I really am just extraordinarily tired of all of this. Just… Do whatever you need to do, speak to whoever you need to speak to. I'm going to talk to you in the morning.

IAN. I really am –

VANESSA. In the morning. Please. Not now.

IAN. Yes. Of course. Sleep, um… sleep well.

Scene ends.

Scene Six

1988. We hear the council election results being announced.

OFFICER. Bilston, Arthur, Conservative party. Seven hundred and forty-three. Cartwright, Shirley, Social and Liberal Democrats, one thousand, one hundred and twenty-one. Foster, Malcolm, Social Democratic party, three hundred and two. Kirkwood, Josie, Labour Party, three thousand, one hundred and eighty-four. Therefore Josie Kirkwood is duly elected as the new councillor for –

The voice fades out, covered by applause. Lights up on DAI *as* JOSIE *enters. Both are smartly dressed.*

DAI. There she is!

JOSIE. Dai!

She embraces him.

DAI. Councillor Kirkwood.

She bows to him.

JOSIE. Councillor Griffiths.

DAI. How do you like the sound of it?

JOSIE. Got quite the ring, I'd say.

DAI. Suits you.

JOSIE. Thank you. Not quite Caesar, but…

DAI. Well, Rome wasn't built in a day.

JOSIE. No.

DAI (*consulting a piece of paper*). Three thousand, one hundred and eighty-four. That's fifty-nine-point-five per cent of total votes cast. That is a three-point-two-per-cent swing in our favour from last time around. That, my dear, is a very satisfactory day at the office.

JOSIE. And on what – twenty-five-per-cent turnout?

DAI (*checks*). Twenty-seven.

JOSIE. Not stellar.

DAI. Perfectly respectable.

JOSIE. Yeah.

DAI. Enjoy it. Enjoy all of this while you can.

JOSIE. Oh, like that is it?

DAI. I didn't mean –

JOSIE. I know.

DAI. Savour the victories, for they can feel few and far between, believe me. I saw your parents were in. Are they proud?

JOSIE. Yeah. Yeah, I think so. Think they'd still rather I had a boyfriend, but –

DAI. They are, trust me.

JOSIE. Hope so.

DAI. You've come a long way, Councillor Kirkwood.

JOSIE. Well, I was guided by the best.

DAI. Ah, too kind. Drink?

JOSIE. I've had a couple already.

DAI. Not driving, are you?

JOSIE. No, but –

DAI. Then I insist. Can you stomach whiskey?

JOSIE. Sure.

DAI. My kind of woman. Coming right up.

DAI pours them two generous glasses.

Cheers.

JOSIE. Cheers.

DAI. To your victory.

JOSIE. To ours. To the Republic!

DAI. Ah, yes.

They chink glasses and drink.

JOSIE (*beginning cautiously*). You know I heard a… I've got
a new nickname, in some circles. With some who aren't still
calling me 'Two Soups'.

DAI. Oh? Nothing – ?

JOSIE. No, nothing bad, nothing… Well, I don't think it is,
really. They call me 'The Project'.

DAI. The Project?

JOSIE. Yeah.

DAI. What does that – ?

JOSIE. 'See her? She's The Project.' 'You're Dai's little Project,
aren't you?'

DAI. I don't think I –

JOSIE. They reckon you're on some Pygmalion kick – we've
got a Henry-Higgins-Eliza-Doolittle thing going on.

DAI. The idle gossip of bored Party members should be –

JOSIE. No, I know. And I wasn't… It didn't upset me.

DAI. Good. Because I'd hate you to think –

JOSIE. No, it's fine, honest, but it got me thinking… I do know
how much you've looked out for me. Had my back. Made
sure I –

DAI. All I've done is –

JOSIE. Is take an interest. Which is a… maybe it shouldn't be,
but it is a big deal, actually, and… And anyway, I got to
thinking that maybe I hadn't really said thank you enough.

DAI. To me?

JOSIE. Yeah.

DAI. What for?

JOSIE. For not just… For taking that interest. For… and I'm
not saying they're right, that I'm your protégée or anything,
I'm not… But if you were going to choose someone to, to

look after you could've done what everyone else does which is just find a younger version of yourself, y'know –

DAI. And who's to say I didn't?

JOSIE. Alright. Yeah, alright. But that's just it, isn't it? You were able to… Oh bollocks, I'm starting to tear up, that's embarrassing – this is why I shouldn't do speeches. Pushing on – all I'm saying is you have been one of the only, more or less the only person to accept on face value that I have a right to be here, and that is actually pretty extraordinary, so, so… So I'm just saying I'm grateful, really. I hope you know how grateful I am, and if you don't then I hope I can find a way to show you. (*Beat.*) Okay, that's it.

She stops. DAI *pulls* JOSIE *towards him and kisses her. It isn't aggressive as such, but it is forceful, and takes* JOSIE *entirely by surprise.*

Dai!

DAI. You're very welcome.

JOSIE (*pulling herself away*). Uh… uh, no, I –

DAI. It's okay.

JOSIE. I'm sorry.

DAI. You've nothing to be sorry for.

JOSIE. No, I didn't –

DAI. No one's here – no one's going to burst in.

JOSIE. No, but… Oh God. I am really sorry, but –

DAI (*amused*). Relax! Relax –

JOSIE. This is my fault. I'm an idiot. I've had a drink, and –

DAI. This is fine. This is allowed.

JOSIE. But I… Look, Dai, you know how much I respect you –

DAI. And I respect you too. I respect you as a colleague –
I respect you as a woman. You're a magnificent woman, Josie.

JOSIE. But I think you misunderstood me.

DAI. I don't think I did.

JOSIE. No, you did, and that's my fault, but –

DAI. 'I hope I can find a way to show you my gratitude'?

JOSIE. Okay, that was –

DAI (*with a chuckle. He's much too physically close*). It's okay! You needn't be so jumpy. Tonight is about celebrating. Tonight is about exciting new partnerships – forging a brighter future. Let me welcome you into the fold, Councillor.

He goes in for another kiss. JOSIE *breaks away.*

JOSIE. I don't think this is a good idea.

DAI. We can go somewhere else.

JOSIE. I don't want this.

DAI. I'm sorry?

JOSIE. I don't… I am really sorry if I led you to believe otherwise, but I'm not interested in you in that way.

DAI. You're not?

JOSIE. I feel awful.

DAI. Right.

JOSIE. I think you're brilliant –

DAI. I think you're not being entirely honest with yourself, are you, Josie?

JOSIE. What do you mean?

DAI. How many times have you slipped into conversation that you don't have a boyfriend?

JOSIE. I…

DAI. That wasn't meant for me?

JOSIE. No! I never –

DAI. You haven't been flirting with me since day one? Answering the door in your nightie – calling me Caesar?

JOSIE. The papers called you Caesar.

DAI. So I'm a fantasist, am I?

JOSIE. No! No, but –

DAI. No, I didn't think so. So don't play the fool. You've put up a good fight – your honour's still intact – but be honest now: you want this.

JOSIE. I don't.

DAI. Josie –

JOSIE. I... I'm going to get that cab. I'm really sorry.

She begins to leave. He calls after her.

DAI. Funny way of expressing your gratitude.

She stops.

But I suppose now you've got what you wanted.

JOSIE. No –

DAI. You... You were nothing when I found you. Do you think it was easy, doing all this – getting you here?

JOSIE. Dai –

DAI. And now you're Lady Muck, are you? Got it made – don't need me any more. Well, good luck to you.

JOSIE. Can I go?

DAI. Go. Go on. See how far you get. Let's see if you can make it ten yards on your own. Stupid woman. Stupid girl. Don't – don't you dare look at me like that! I am not a bad man. I know who the bad men are – I know what the bad men look like. And you want to line me up beside them? If you had any idea... I work endlessly, tirelessly, I go against my brothers, and for what? To be painted as a monster? Am I not owed anything? Should I not be rewarded? A man who works without recompense is a slave! I shall not be indentured! I am not duty-bound to fight the fights you cannot win yourselves and be spat on for my efforts. I am not a bad man! But I am a man, yes, and for you that is enough to condemn me. You make enemies of your allies because we can never be good enough for you and that is why you are nowhere! Go. Just get out.

Scene ends.

Scene Seven

2018. VANESSA present. IAN enters with two takeaway coffees. IAN is tentative, VANESSA is exhausted, her tone initially more subdued-snarky than openly aggressive.

IAN. Knock knock.

VANESSA. Who's there? Oh, it's the Grim-Up-North Reaper.

IAN. Brought you coffee.

VANESSA (*taking it*). Thanks.

IAN. Think I've finally learnt your order.

VANESSA. Yeah, well it's a skinny latte, isn't it? It's not Fermat's Last Theorem.

IAN (*choosing to ignore this*). You sleep?

VANESSA. What do you think?

IAN. Tough, um, tough night all round. Tough campaign. Lots of...

VANESSA. He's not going to do it.

IAN. Hmm?

VANESSA. Jerry. He's going to get a lot closer than he should, it'll be embarrassing, and ultimately it is going to weaken my mandate a little, but he's not actually going to beat me.

IAN. I see.

VANESSA. But you knew that already.

IAN. Respectfully –

VANESSA. Ah yes, always very respectful.

IAN. I think that's wishful… I think that's underestimating just
how damaging –

VANESSA. Yeah, well, what do you know?

IAN. This isn't what I want either.

VANESSA. Right.

IAN. It isn't.

VANESSA. No. No, you must be heartbroken, I'm sure.
Dreaming of this moment ever since you were a little girl.

IAN (*struggling to stay scrupulously polite*). This isn't… I beg
you, please try to appreciate this is bigger than you. We want
– everybody *wanted* this to work with you. Of course we did.
We did everything –

VANESSA. Really?

IAN. Yes, very bloody really. You might not have noticed, but
there are a lot of us round here who haven't been sleeping
much lately.

VANESSA (*dryly*). Well thank you for your service.

IAN. Everything was done; rigged the deck for you every way
we could, cleared out the serious competition, put up with
endless, endless… Because the word from on high was 'this
is our girl' – here's the one who ticks someone's set of boxes.
Fine – I'm a good soldier – I can follow orders. But
whatever we tried, it wasn't enough. So here we are, day
after day, hour after hour, furiously polishing this sorry turd
of a campaign, and all the while you're acting like you're the
only one whose shit doesn't stink.

VANESSA. Sorry to have been such a burden.

IAN. Except you're not, are you?

VANESSA. Not really, no.

IAN. No. You still think the world's out to get you. You still
think this is everyone's fault but your own. And worst of all,
you think you're better – smarter – funnier – more advanced

– than anyone else in this bloody county, including everyone you want to vote for you.

VANESSA. So what?

IAN. Excuse me?

VANESSA. So what if I am?

IAN. Am what?

VANESSA. Better. Cleverer. That's a bad thing, is it? When did that become…? Don't you want the best people as your leaders? Shouldn't they be your betters? Isn't that why you put them in charge?

IAN. So now you're just openly admitting it?

VANESSA. You're damn right I am! Why shouldn't I? To get to where I am today it has been an absolute necessity to always be the smartest person at the table. That's the bare minimum. And – here's the kicker – and it's equally crucial that no one at the table ever acknowledge it. To get in the room with the white men you have to be twice as clever as any of them, but to stay there you have to play dumb. Well I wasn't going to do that this time.

IAN. And look where it's got you.

VANESSA. And that's on me?

IAN. Has it ever crossed your mind, Vanessa, that people don't like you not because you're a woman, but because you're a stuck-up bitch?

VANESSA. Oh fuck you!

IAN. Touché.

VANESSA. Yes. Fuck you. Fuck you right up the decommissioned mineshaft. I am not – I was never the problem here.

IAN. No?

VANESSA. No, sir. So fuck you and all the other butt-hurt old white men who hear one woman speaking and scream that they're being silenced. Fuck you and your little-England

backward-looking Brexit-voting salt-of-the-earth ever-so-
'umble insidiously sexist, racist, no-I-listen-to-Elton-John-so
-I-can't-be-homophobic, not-got-an-issue-with-Muslims-so-
long-as-they-don't-look-act-or-sound-like-Muslims
post-colonial, patriarchal bullshit.

IAN. Right.

VANESSA. Fuck the lot of you.

IAN. That's how it is, is it?

VANESSA. Uh-huh.

IAN. Well then, respectfully, fuck you too.

VANESSA. Okay.

IAN. Fuck you and all your beard-sculpting gap-year trust-fund
gender-variant spiralised-avocado snapchat Shoreditch
snowflake friends.

VANESSA. Wow.

IAN. Every last one.

VANESSA. How would you even spiralise an avocado? Jesus!

IAN (*ignoring this*). You – I can't believe you're the ones we're
courting! You're our future? You're the next generation of
Labour leaders? God help us. You don't have a clue what we
stand for – what we've been through. You share a dozen
online petitions a day but we've got to walk over hot coals
before you'll register to vote. You'll spend two hours
queueing for a burger but you've never seen a picket line.
You are the most entitled –

VANESSA. We're entitled?

IAN. You only love Socialism because you think it means
you'll get everything for free. Sorry, sweetheart, Labour
means graft. Real work. Honest work. Not sat around
drinking your four-pound lattes and wondering why you're
always broke.

VANESSA. Right. Okay, right. No, this is… Okay, so firstly –
lattes, still? Honestly? Seriously, of all the… Lattes are still

your signifier of wacky millennial excess? This is slumming it.
We drink cold-brew. We drink aeropress. We drink kombucha.

IAN. What in God's name is – ?

VANESSA. I don't know! None of us know, and it's disgusting,
but we drink it anyway, because we're all awful, awful
people. No one in Shoreditch has drunk a latte since 1993.
Ask me why. Go on – ask me.

IAN. Why?

VANESSA. Because we're all lactose-intolerant, motherfucker!
Every last one of us. That's right, my generation is so
goddamn sensitive we're even triggered by dairy. You happy?

IAN. I'm not sure I –

VANESSA. And secondly – secondly, because this is the real
point – we're entitled? Us? When you graduated – if you'd
graduated, sorry – a terraced house here cost under five
grand. No student debt. Plenty of jobs – jobs for life. You
had it made! My generation didn't tank the economy, it
didn't invade Iraq, it didn't flog off the NHS and stoke petty
nationalism. So if my generation looks at the state of politics
today and doesn't exactly wet their knickers in excitement,
can you blame us?

IAN. So why are you here?

VANESSA. To make things better!

IAN. Right.

VANESSA. And at this point I don't really give a toss if you
believe me.

IAN. Oh, I do. No, I genuinely do.

VANESSA. Okay.

IAN. And nothing gets better without us – without Labour in
power.

VANESSA. Yes, but only –

IAN. No buts. Bottom line. So egos aside –

VANESSA. Labour can't win if it won't change.

IAN. We were doing just fine here.

VANESSA. Not all of us.

IAN. You should've stuck where you were.

VANESSA. You need someone like me here.

IAN. Like a hole in the head.

VANESSA. How much of this did you plan?

IAN. I'm sorry?

VANESSA. I'm just wondering how much. Was it from the word go? When they announced the shortlist? The first time you heard my name – saw my picture?

IAN. What're you talking about?

VANESSA. Because it is going to be you, isn't it? The last-minute replacement. Local lad, everyone's mate, safe pair of hands. I made some enquiries of my own.

IAN. Don't be daft.

VANESSA. Did you put Jerry up to it, or just decide to take advantage?

IAN. You think I engineered all this?

VANESSA. Because he'll step aside now, won't he – if I'm gone? Or ease off, anyway. He won't have a problem with you.

IAN. I knew you had a persecution complex, but I didn't realise you were this paranoid.

VANESSA. And you knew, didn't you, all about Simon and the working group right from the start. That's why you pushed so hard on steel – forced me into it because you knew it'd come back to bite me. Am I really so dangerous? Is the thought of having a woman of colour leading your precious city really so abhorrent that you'd go to these lengths?

IAN. For the last time –

VANESSA. What's wrong with me?

IAN. You're not one of us. (*Beat.*) You're not. Not race, not sex, none of that – couldn't give a monkey's. Not one of the tribe. You don't belong. What's worse, you don't want to. You don't want to represent the people here, you just want to mould them in your image. Well I say they're fine as they are. And I know this is a very unpopular view to hold in the twenty-first century, but I say being white and male doesn't automatically make you a criminal. We don't all need shipping off for re-education.

VANESSA. I never said you did.

IAN. But it's what you think. I'm not the one with the prejudice, I'm not the one obsessed with… 'We need more women! We need more minorities! This is a national disgrace!' Why? Why does it matter?

VANESSA. Why do we need a representative government?

IAN. If you like.

VANESSA. I can't believe we're seriously still on this.

IAN. Why not just the best person for the job? Why not keep it that simple?

VANESSA. I am the best!

IAN. For this? For here? You seriously think…? You can rail against the patriarchy until the cows come home, but all it's done to you so far is bump you up the queue – you'd be nowhere without it.

VANESSA. Wow. Just wow. Okay.

IAN. Am I wrong?

VANESSA. You can… Look, you go ahead and believe whatever lets you sleep at night, but don't imagine for a second that if I had a cock between my legs I wouldn't have got here twice as fast and twice as easily.

IAN. They can just deselect you, you know.

VANESSA. Hmm?

IAN. It's easier for everyone – less embarrassing all round – if you stand down quietly, but we can just take you off the ballot.

VANESSA. Right.

IAN. Vote of no confidence. We'd have the numbers.

VANESSA. I'm sure.

IAN. And then you're really screwed. You go out like that, you don't get to walk back in.

VANESSA. Yes.

IAN. So finish your latte. Have a think. Try to… This was never right for you. Never a good fit. Doesn't mean there won't be… So take it like a man and try and be a bit sensible, alright? (*Beat.*) Alright then.

IAN *begins to leave.*

VANESSA (*after him*). Do you really not know why?

IAN (*stopping*). Why what?

VANESSA. Why it matters. Why it being me matters?

IAN. No.

VANESSA. It's because you represent. (*Beat.*) If you represent you can inspire. But you need to be there – to be held up – to be visible. It isn't arrogance, or ego, they need to see me – people like me – because how else is anyone who doesn't look like you ever going to get anywhere? And you'll still be there too, just not in every seat. I'm needed, and I need to be the best, because I show the best can look like anything. Otherwise we'll lose them – our next generation of brightest minds – we do ourselves untold damage if we keep passing on this message that the future doesn't look like them. Who can they see? Where are they? What do they look like? There are some – yes, I know there are some – and yes of course we're all very inspired by Diane Abbott but if your list only runs to one name then you've still got problems.

And I'm not dismissing anyone. I'm not saying I can't… I am Atlee. I am Bevan. Keir Hardie. Tony Benn. Fuck – Tony Blair – a little bit. I'll own up to a little bit of Tony. I'll take a bit of Wilson and a bit of Kinnock and a bit of Smith. I will step into the shoes of Barbara Castle and Mo Mowlam and

Betty Boothroyd – I will fill my boots with them. And yeah – and Diane – I will go to war behind Diane any day of the week, never doubt it. But it isn't enough.

During the next section of the speech she might start to gradually change into her JOSIE *costume.*

So do you know what I did – what I had to do? I made someone up. I built this woman from scratch – the role model I'd never had. I made her about my mum's age, so she could pick a fight with Thatcher, this proper working-class hero, this brilliant, down-to-earth, far more street cred than I ever… I called her Josie, because that was my granny's name, and I never really knew her but she sounded great. And she would – the thing is it would've been so much tougher, back in the eighties, climbing an even bigger hill, so every time something really shitty happened to me I'd imagine something worse happening to her, and she'd get over it, so why couldn't I?

And that's crazy. That can't be right – that my most inspirational figure is someone I had to invent. And you know the really tragic thing? When I picture her back then she's not Prime Minister, not even an MP, just a councillor. Just keeps her head down and gets shat on constantly and slogs, just slogs away, one step forward, two steps back, but I'd imagine – and this is mad, I know – but I'd imagine meeting her now, once the election's over, and I'd shake her hand, and she'd say, 'I never dreamt someone like us would end up running all of this.' And I wouldn't even have to thank her because she'd know – she'd just know.

Look, this is… Fuck it. This is an election no one wanted for a role nobody understands, but if me doing this, if being visible, if all that means some other little girl doesn't have to go to the lengths of making someone up then all of this… all of this… Don't you see? That's why it matters.

IAN (*not unkindly*). Well. Better luck next time.

IAN *goes.*

Scene Eight

1988. The city council. A session is about to begin where JOSIE *will give her maiden speech.*

DAI. So then – ready for your first day of school?

JOSIE. I… Yeah. Ready as I'll ever be.

DAI. Good, good.

A silence.

I don't think anything needs to be awkward between us, do you?

JOSIE. No.

DAI. No regrets, no hard feelings. We're all on the same side, after all.

JOSIE. Yeah.

DAI. I wanted to try and put you at ease, in that regard.

JOSIE. Thank you.

DAI. There's all sorts goes on in these halls after hours. Although of course the more enlightened know not to believe a word of it.

JOSIE. Right.

DAI (*a little more pointedly*). They know not to listen to any nonsense.

JOSIE. Yeah. Good. No, that's good to know.

Pause.

DAI. So. So you've nothing to worry about. I wouldn't want you thinking… I'll always be very glad that I could help you – could give you the extra leg-up when you needed it. Proud that I could do that.

JOSIE. Right.

DAI. So crack a smile. You made it.

JOSIE. The real work starts now.

DAI. That's the spirit, sister. (*Puts his hand on her, perhaps giving her shoulder a squeeze. It's definitely unpleasant.*) And I'll always be in your corner – right behind you – don't forget that.

JOSIE. I won't.

DAI. Good. (*Beat.*) All set? No props, no costumes?

JOSIE. No, just me.

DAI. No talk of tea and empire?

JOSIE. Maybe a little.

DAI. I'd keep things simple, if I were you. Just tell them who you are.

JOSIE. But that is who I am.

DAI. You know what happens when you overthink things.

JOSIE. Yeah.

DAI. There'll be time for grand narratives and great oratory, today just… 'very humbled – thank you to the leadership – illustrious history – rising to the challenges ahead.' You know, all the old classics.

JOSIE. Right.

DAI. Attagirl. You'll knock 'em dead. Shall we?

He gestures for her to follow him.

JOSIE. Dai?

DAI (*stopping*). Yes?

JOSIE. Thank you.

DAI. You don't have to –

JOSIE (*with a steeliness*). For bringing me to the fight. For showing me how much there still is to do.

DAI (*forcing a smile*). My pleasure, sister.

JOSIE. I won't forget it, I promise you.

A snap into –

Scene Nine

2018. Now IAN *and* VANESSA *are before each other.*

IAN. You ready?

VANESSA. Not really.

IAN. They'll give you a good send-off. We're all very grateful. Everyone's very grateful.

VANESSA. Right.

IAN. Everyone gets it – what you put into this. Just wasn't the right –

VANESSA. Can you…? Sorry, I think it's just actually much worse when you try to be nice about it.

IAN. As you wish. Best get it over with then.

Lights shift as VANESSA *approaches a podium, presumably to make a concession speech.*

VANESSA. Thank you. Thanks. I'll try to keep this quick. This is a great city. It deserves great leadership – clear, unified leadership. Leadership that honours the past, looks to the future, challenges at every opportunity the idea that our best days are behind us. And that requires a leader who can give it everything, who can commit one hundred per cent. As some of you may know, my mother… my mother has been, uh… Sorry. Sorry. (*Pauses, draws breath. Makes her decision.*) My mother used to say, 'A woman is like a teabag – you never know how strong she is until you put her in hot water.' I'm more of a coffee person myself, but I like the sentiment. And I am stronger than you know, believe me. I'm not going anywhere. I'm going to make something of this. Because that's what we do – we're makers – we make things here. Things that are useful and beautiful, necessary and revolutionary. For everyone who came before me and everyone who'll come after. For every name that's been forgotten and every name you never knew. That's why I'm here. That's who I am. That's why I belong. Now, does anyone have any questions?

Blackout.

End.

A Nick Hern Book

Steel first published in Great Britain as a paperback original in 2018 by Nick Hern Books Limited, The Glasshouse, 49a Goldhawk Road, London W12 8QP, in association with Sheffield Theatres

Steel copyright © 2018 Chris Bush

Chris Bush has asserted her right to be identified as the author of this work

Cover design: Craig Fleming

Designed and typeset by Nick Hern Books, London
Printed in Great Britain by Mimeo Ltd, Huntingdon, Cambridgeshire PE29 6XX

A CIP catalogue record for this book is available from the British Library

ISBN 978 1 84842 771 6

Woodland
CARBON
www.woodlandcarbon.co.uk
NICK HERN BOOKS
Printed on Carbon Captured paper